T0194257

In the
Country
of Men

Also by Jan L. Waldron

Giving Away Simone

In
the
Country
of Men

My Travels

Jan L. Waldron

ANCHOR BOOKS

DOUBLEDAY

New York   London   Toronto   Sydney   Auckland

AN ANCHOR BOOK
PUBLISHED BY DOUBLEDAY
a division of Bantam Doubleday Dell Publishing Group, Inc.
1540 Broadway, New York, New York 10036

ANCHOR BOOKS, DOUBLEDAY, and the portrayal of an anchor are
trademarks of Doubleday, a division of Bantam Doubleday Dell
Publishing Group, Inc.

In the Country of Men: My Travels was originally published in hardcover by
Anchor Books in 1997.

A Dialogue of Self and Soul, II, st. 1, reprinted with the permission of Simon
& Schuster from *The Poems of W. B. Yeats: A New Edition*, edited by
Richard J. Finneran. Copyright 1933 by Macmillan Publishing Company;
copyright renewed © 1961 by Bertha Georgie Yeats.

The lines from "Orion" copyright © 1993 by Adrienne Rich. Copyright ©
1969 by W.W. Norton & Company, Inc., from *Collected Early Poems: 1950–
1970* by Adrienne Rich. Reprinted by permission of the author
and W.W. Norton & Company, Inc.

Book design by Maria Carella

The Library of Congress has cataloged the Anchor hardcover edition
of this work as follows:
Waldron, Jan L.
In the country of men: my travels / by Jan L. Waldron.
p.   cm.
1. Men—United States.   2. Sex role—United States.   3. Waldron,
Jan L.   I. Title.
HQ1090.3W353   1997
305.3—dc20   96-34894
CIP

ISBN 978-0-385-48565-4

Printed in the United States of America

145052501

For my father and his grandsons, K., P., and R.

Acknowledgments

I would like to thank Merrill Black, Susan Nichols, Lorraine Neville, Lisa Horwitz, Eleanor Majewski, Janet LaBelle, and Fran Alamia for being girlfriends extraordinaire; my brother for teaching me a lot of what I know and love about boys; Elizabeth Hall-Moitoza for her life-altering wisdom and warm humor; my birthdaughter Rebecca Carroll for loving with me the boys, her brothers; Jay Schadler for Saturday-night suppers and road stories; my agents Susan Raihofer for her staggering smarts and ceaseless energy and David Black for his enduring faith and for asking, "Where are the guys?" (Here are the guys); my editors Martha Levin for her enthusiastic interest and Tina Pohlman for her guidance and excellent suggestions throughout.

I am grateful to David McPhail for being the best there ever was.

And, for the hope, I have my sons to thank.

Contents

Prologue

I have spent all but two and a half years of my forty-five-year life living, voluntarily and involuntarily, with males—a brother and father, roommates, lovers, and sons. I can say nothing in general about the experience except that adult males are significantly limited in ways that are important to me, but that ultimately I am optimistic about boys; and that the times I was living alone or with other women were notable for their equitable ease and the stunning lack of detail management.

When I was eleven, my mother broke down and our family fell apart. When I think back to when our home was crumbling, I cannot find my father. When I look hard, his appearance is vague; he is hiding like a kid caught in a jam. Back then it never occurred to me to expect or ask for his help. I seemed to know even then that the challenge before him had exceeded his abilities, though I was lovingly captivated by my father before the fall.

It is my father's withholding, his failure to act or give, that emerges in the recollection and has left me muttering to myself most of my life: Can a guy confront the difficult, uncomfortably complex, the untidy terrain of emotions, without aggressively deflecting the heat or eying the exit signs? Is there a man on the planet (besides a highly paid professional) who can say, "Let's talk about this," sit relatively still, keep his feet on the floor, and bravely, unflinchingly stay the course—from tantrum to ecstasy, from intimacy to rage—without speechlessly plotting an escape?

But my brother revealed possibilities. As a young sister I remember witnessing the trials he faced as a boy to be a boy. In our suburban fifties neighborhood it was expected that he would want to fist-fight, chase and tease girls. But my affectionate brother wanted to read, not wrestle; his tears came easily and often; he was sensitive to his surroundings, gentle and thoughtful with his sister. Why, I remember thinking, would anyone want *him* to fit into *that*—the constricting, hormone-defined tomb of so-called boyhood?

I saw the attempted social genderfication of my brother as infuriating unadulterated dumbness. I got mad young at the constraints of gender.

Having been oriented to a charming man's unreliability but to a boy's promise and vulnerabilities, I seek men who embody some of all: men who give freely and often, are unapologetically romantic, men who celebrate her flight inasmuch as it does not collide with his high-maintenance flying. Men who could have, in another generation, in another place, been fully realized. I am seduced by their fertile, fragile yearning to love and be loved, to be released from the ill fit of prescribed manhood and the absence of their own distant father's blessing. While they reject the myths, they are less certain where to look for replacements, except in the eyes of the women whose love they are sure will deliver them.

I had always hoped I would have sons; and have always been grateful that I did. My brother and I had been inseparable;

loving a boy, up close, seemed natural. In my adult life I have not had the privilege of sustained female kinship, save for a grandmother whose true value I realized only after her death, because I had relied too long on her daughter's embittered translations. And my relationship with my birthdaughter Rebecca, the child I gave away and whom I have known for the past sixteen years, has been volatile in the extreme. We have been, off and on, allies, strangers, admirers, and confidantes; our interaction is regulated by our shared experience of her adoption, which has left us both wounded and spent. We are so emotionally entangled that we expect and each regularly grants the other emotional furloughs. My mother, whom I have seen only twice in the last twelve years, sends sporadic, muddled letters to which I rarely want or am able to respond.

It is impossible to know what kind of ties I might have had with my female relatives were our circumstances not infected by distrust—if I had not surrendered my daughter to other parents, if my mother had not left me. But, in the broad view, boys seemed simpler.

When my sons were four and five their father and I separated. He retreated, and I became their sole parent, once again doing the work because a man would not. Over the years people have told me only a father can make a man of a boy. Certainly a man can help. My response as the mother of sons is not to gather a prospective panel of jurors to prove a boy's manhood, but rather to give my sons the ability to anoint themselves. "You tell me," I want to say, "are you man enough? *You* decide." It is a tentative enterprise to depend on the judgments of others who are still searching to signify another's soul. I have always balked at the generally held belief that boys without in-house fathers are destined to be deficient; a belief based on the presumption that existing manhood is worthy of inheritance. I am convinced that, despite their father's distance, boys can be good fathers, compassionate friends, and women-ready men. Given the skills and training—of reflection and instincts—a boy can travel the paths he plots for himself; and then decide if he loves who he sees himself to be, so-called manhood be damned.

I rarely take notes and have never been able to keep up with a journal. When I have attempted it, I found that tallying up the day, once removed, left a disingenuous distance between me and the life being lived. The journal-keeper's take was invasive.

I prefer the unforgettable to the continually fashioned chronicle. Whatever details or experiences can be summoned over the long haul have probably earned their place among our remembrances for better or worse for one reason or another. Looking back without liner notes provides an organic editing process and feels, if not more accurate, at least more authentic.

I have never looked at my sons as sociological events. When I am a mother to them I am in far too deep, blindly wired to my instincts, to quantify or study them. What I write here is what has risen into view, after the fact, the impressions that have stayed. Nor do I live through my children, to fill out a woman's thin life. But I do live much of my life for them, for now.

The cluttered, hopeful, and hopeless history I have with men has informed a deep consideration of what I can expect from men and what, if any, obligation I have to help my sons become men. I emerge from my experiences convinced that manhood, as we've come to know and ambivalently accept it, does not exist per se. It's a hilarious error and makes me laugh, when I am not observing the aching elusiveness of the hunt.

In these pages, I consider the pose of masculinity with an advantage males do not have. As a woman I witness male behavior unhindered by the piercing gaze of the brotherhood; and as a mother I see the vulnerabilities of the uninitiated. I observe in the males around me both a hapless struggle to conform to an impossible model and a yearning to be freed of the pursuit. Some members of the men's movement have exacerbated an already frustrating chase by making of manhood conversion a religious experience, indeed a myth. In his book *Iron John,* Robert Bly seems to be shaking his brethren until their teeth rattle because he is so let down by their failure to find middle ground. He mocks the isolated, callous man of the fifties, and the "soft," eager-to-please male that emerged in the seventies. Surely both personae are limited. But when he could have taken the search to higher ground, Bly does to men and their manhood what has been done, uselessly, all along: he holds them accountable for an unachievable, mysterious "deep masculinity."

What we do not need more of are inflexible, divine definitions and unattainable aspirations. There is no key under the pillow, no transformative voodoo, that can or should take the place of the simple, tough work we do to become and be. Elevating our human journeys to superhuman heights, making figures of fathers, institutionalizing motherhood, and myths of manhood have left us all feeling slightly and consistently incomplete. Our perceived inadequacies, none more so than in men, have done us in. The quest for manhood entails a search for *selfhood;* it is an ongoing, interior venture.

Without the training, men will continue to hunt for an elusive credential, fumbling, flooding, lost, and hungry—blind to the fortune within. Only when boys and men provide their own benedictions will they be full enough, able and willing to lovingly sponsor the journeys of others—their sons, daughters, lovers, friends, sisters, and mothers.

In his ingratiating, cynical handbook about male-female relations, *Men Are From Mars, Women Are From Venus,* author John Gray panders to and fails to question existing inferior roles. He talks about one gender "scoring points" with the other. By urging men to tell their women they are pretty, by advising women to admire their men, he sets the humanist cause back about a century. Is he suggesting we train our daughters in the unique needs of egocentric men and our sons to be aware of a fragile woman's special desires? Behavior modification, vis-à-vis genders, is where we've been and it hasn't been good for us. We cannot expect intergender coddling to do the work only unisex self-awareness can. Gray, and his ilk, gleefully accommodate and cash in on contrived gender types.

In writing this book, I have had to confront tough personal truths about the males in my life. I have had to put on the 3-D glasses, stifle the gender jokes, haul out and take a hard look at what I had become all too willing to file under Hopeless or Absurd. I have revisited a history of disillusion and discovered a world of hope, both of which I am convinced I would not have found or figured out had I not had sons. And it has been a harrowing enlightenment—to discover how much the other gender has meant and continues to mean to me, when I would have, in years before, said it was peripheral.

Finally, I write here now with males in mind, hoping never to write about or contemplate, emphatically, the issues of gender again.

My brother and I used to joke that my chief contribution to twentieth-century America would be an attempt to raise two males who would pick up their dirty socks. I set my sights low. My older son is aggressively untidy; my younger son less so. But worse, I've started leaving my used socks on top of my sneakers after a walk, and sometimes in the hall before my showers. I like the gust of air on yawning, tired toes; and then walking away, leaving a trail, gratifyingly absorbed in cause, disinterested, for the moment, in effect. I *get* that now. I'm not sure what this means, except perhaps that I have had far less of an influence on my sons than I ever could have imagined they would have on me.

Whatever disappointment I carry from having outlived an intimate trail of letdowns proffered by men near and far is blurred by the golden glare of faith I have in boys, the men of a new generation. I am convinced the gods gave me sons because they knew I was close to giving up hope for a better brand of male. Without having had male children, I imagine I would be murmuring loudly to myself by now, finding men to fix and still failing, perhaps eventually reaching a languid truce with them all.

"We will give you two male children," the gods whisper from above, "whom you will love in the extreme; in their faces find the prisms." I look and it changes my life.

—JAN L. WALDRON

In the
Country
of Men

That toil of growing up;
The ignominy of boyhood; the distress
Of boyhood changing into man;
The unfinished man and his pain.

—W. B. YEATS

Part 1
Father

*The memory of things gone is important to a jazz musician. Things
like old folks singing in the moonlight in the backyard on a hot
night or something someone said long ago.*

—DUKE ELLINGTON

1

Aside from the brief relief it can bring on hot days, I have never liked swimming much. When I was young I was petrified of the mystery of dark bodies of water—lakes in particular. I thought if I went too far out or too deep in I would be pulled down and buried alive by pounds of unforgiving liquid. I have always loved being at the ocean, and on the shore of a lake, but the water is no friend of mine.

Our family's trips to Thayer Beach were special occasions. My father knew the owner of the private beach from his days as a camp counselor, so we were admitted free and felt like honored guests, one of the fancy folks who could afford a place on the sprawling white sand. Platinum-haired Lana Turner look-alikes posed under striped umbrellas; men suntanned and slept; children wrapped in vinyl animals played at the edge of the lake. This was a perfect yellow, warm summer day.

About an hour after consuming our chicken salad sandwiches and cherry Kool-Aid, my father had come out of the water and invited me into the lake, which glittered from the afternoon sun. I was five or six. He knew I was uneasy in the water, but it was hot and he wanted to help bring me out of my fear, so he urged me to try the slide. He would catch me, he promised. "But, Dad," I remember saying, "what if I slide down too fast, and you can't?" "That won't happen," he said. "I promise."

When I was a kid, I would linger unsurely in the shallow edge of the lake, while my brother and mother eagerly waded past me into the deep water beyond. They could not wait to lie down in the water, submerge their heads, and swim and swim until they were sunlit spots, hundreds of yards beyond the beach-bound crowd. Looking back, I realize my father, like me, was less comfortable in the water. He loved our lake; but he floated on his back and kicked, got wet, and got out. I never saw him actually swim. Maybe it was his own uneasiness that made him, on this day, want to cure mine. Together we would coast out of our fear.

My father stood near the edge of the blanket where I sat between my mother and grandmother, who were sorting food and drinks in a cooler and covering my sun-baked legs. He confidently countered my nervous doubts about taking the plunge. He promised, he said again, to catch me. Finally, I believed. As fearsome as this out-of-control-slip-into-the-water-below might be, I wanted more to have faith in my father. I was ready to risk it all on my dad's promise. I took his hand as we walked over to the looming slide, which seemed to jut into the clouds. From the water below, my father watched carefully as I stepped tentatively up to the top behind fearless dripping boys, eager for another turn.

I sat at the top of the glaring metal chute and stalled; and then, with trust and fright poured into my open-armed parent, who stood in the water below, I let go. I flew into the lake, dunking my father and me with the force of my slide; we fumbled for each other under the water. I panicked and hunted for his arms, he searched for mine. He found me, I grabbed his neck, and with quick strength he pulled me up out of the water. I sobbed and choked and blamed. I fought to get out of his hold.

My father's face constricted with regret. He tried smiling, and said the surprise was mutual. I left him in the water, alone, as I stumbled up onto the sand to find my mother's lap. I felt both betrayed and traitorous. I should've waited for him, taken his comfort. My grandmother and mother wrapped me up in warm towels and rocked me. He stayed behind for a few minutes, recovering without anyone's comfort from having swallowed water too, and having lost his daughter's trust. *Temporarily.* But for years after, he kidded me about it, whenever I doubted him about anything. "I think it was that slide incident," he cajoled, hoping I would disprove his semiserious hunch.

But I didn't.

Obviously, what happened at the beach forty years ago did not dislodge my trust in men forever. But what is striking about our slide mishap are the feelings of that day; they have revisited me a hundred times since in matters of men. I know he wanted to catch me, but he couldn't; how could he know it couldn't be done? Why must a man feel obliged to hold himself to heroic plans? To prove . . . what? That he is the warrior he wishes he were or the savior we need him to be, only to be deluged by our collective longing and impossible hope?

The letdown that day was as much his as mine. When he failed to fulfill the promise, he was undone. I saw it in his face. Looking back, I wish I had taken his hand as we left the water, the scene of his dampened pride. But, oh, if he had caught me and lifted me up in splendid proof . . .

2

"It is our job to convey to you as clearly as we can and as convincingly as possible what we know to be true: that our father wants to die," I declared, in the company of half a dozen medical officials, including doctors and ethicists, my brother, and our virtual spouses.

My father had left an informal but clear living will. "I do not want to be sustained by life support when there is little or no brain activity, assuming one can tell," he wrote in the days before he was all but blind, in crude letters that climbed up and down the page.

In 1993, twenty-five years after the dissolution of our family, after a long but ultimately troubled union with another woman, and after years of alienation from but a final closeness with his children, my father had been stopped in his tracks by a jolt to his brain. He had had a stroke and was left without speech, decorum, even a trace of his charm or gentle wit. He lay idle and out of it in intensive care. His soft piano-playing hands, which had never been under the hood of a car or seen hard labor, were bent into useless angles on his chest, which heaved erratically.

My brother was out of town and I was at a friend's house for dinner in another state when, in his small, sparse, dark apartment, he suffered his last and worst indignity. A neighbor, who had agreed to check in on him, found him on his bed dazed, mute, and disheveled. Imagining him alone and horrified during his final conscious minutes hurts and haunts me still.

We did not want rehabilitation, feeding tubes, or medication for our dying father. My brother agitated, and argued philosophies of treatment. He was occasionally outraged, often loud. After he got their attention and the doctors knew our family was firmly aligned, I began my dispassionate plea.

During the last two weeks of our father's life, Clay and I were doing what we did best together—we were a seasoned team of adults-in-crisis caretakers. We became conscientious communicators who carried out our father's plan with the gracious efficacy of veteran diplomats.

By the time we met with doctors, a week after his stroke, our father had been moved out of his bed and was strapped upright into a chair, bobbing tentatively, unknowingly, gurgling incomprehensibles into the air. This was progress, they said. His skin had turned gray and his eyes, dull and repulsed, seemed to be stunned by an interior agony. His johnny covered his small sharp body like a sheet draped on a piece of junk Deco furniture. He had tried twice to pull the IV needle out of his arm and had left a bleeding mess.

My father had been vain about his weight, simply skipped supper and went to the movies if he had gained an extra pound. He did not smoke, drank rarely and then only moderately, prepared freshly squeezed orange juice every morning, played tennis for as long as he could see the ball, exercised his brain in cutthroat Scrabble tournaments, and never, ever, overworked himself. He could still play the piano until the end, though less accurately in the last couple of years.

Glaucoma had claimed his sight about five years before and he was as infuriated and bitter as a well-mannered person could be. For a man whose every day began with an eager reading of the sports page and obits, and who craved independence and privacy and loved nothing more than playing the piano, losing his sight and the use of his hands was a mean ending. He, of the bon mot, the truly quick pun, had been rendered mute and unresponsive.

3

You gotta love a guy who goes AWOL for a hot bath.

In our family during the early years, my father was the romance figure, whose flaws—of cheapness, idleness, and emotional reserve—were forgiven by his eccentricities and the gift of his exquisite piano playing. Though he shared little of his past, the few but amusing stories that emerged endeared him to us all.

My father found the Army a nuisance, we heard, and the war in general absurd. He skipped out twice for reasons less than gallant. The first time was when he got caught in the rain in New York. He was cold, wet, and wanted a bath, and though he had orders to return to his ship by 6 P.M., when he was invited to take a warm tub at a friend's house in Queens, he couldn't resist and bathed straight through his curfew. The other time he did not follow orders was in Normandy, shortly after D-Day, when he went in search, again, of gratification—coffee ice cream. The war was over, he figured, treat time.

In addition to prioritizing his pleasures, he refused to load his gun. A record of this fact helped my brother win a conscientious objector deferment during the Vietnam War; the authorities surmised that peculiar yet committed dovishness ran in the family. My father was disinterested in the pose and underpinnings of the masculine, had no taste for John Wayne, westerns, or wrestling. He played croquet, tennis, and softball—he crossed his legs, never burped audibly or wore a tie. He had no interest in hockey, football, or hunting—primitive, he would say.

My father was the only and unwelcome child of a busy bridge-playing mother and her businessman husband—facts revealed by my mother; my father never spoke of his parents. In the large oval-framed pictures he kept over his bed until he was seventy years old, his parents look composed and fashionable. He said years later that he could not recall their affection. He remembered fondly his wheelchair-bound grandmother who lived with the family until her death when my father was twelve. He would climb up on her chair and they would talk baseball and movies and she would kiss him good night.

After the war he returned to civilian life committed to living simply and sanely, in pursuit of as much personal comfort as he could manage. He played jazz for small fees with friends in a band on weekends, bowled, and dated women. He ran in the Boston Marathon; but years later we joked about this. Noting our father's lust for value, we were sure he ran the twenty-six miles for the free beef stew buffet granted runners who finished, which he did.

What sparse employment he gained in adult life was the result of well-meaning family friends who, it was assumed, would look in on the boy after the death of his parents when he was in his early twenties. He lived in the house and held on tightly to the inheritance his parents had bequeathed him (as if it were their warm arms), knowing he wasn't likely to pursue conventional work and would need the income over the long haul to subsidize his lack of ambition.

He enjoyed the comforts of his class—college, day trips in fancy cars, and in the summer of 1949, for the fifth year, a job coaching tennis at a family friend's camp in New Hampshire. He was thirty-one and unserious, reluctant to settle down. He spent days teaching privileged girls in tennis skirts the art of swift returns and the importance of steady wrists; and nights skinny dipping in the moonlight with other camp counselors who had rolling blond waves and long athletic limbs.

The year before he died we talked often over dinner about

his summers in the country—twilight softball games, fresh corn, convertibles, unalloyed joy. He grew to know the summer people who lived in comfortable wooden cottages on the edges of huge fields filled with thistles, swallows, bugs, and the sunny haze of summer. The quiet, what the summer folks came to get, betrayed the activity in the plains below, where the year-round residents worked hard and played vigorously.

My father had joined a softball team down on the plains, and one day in July he met the girl he would marry. They spent the rest of the summer together, and when he returned to his parents' house in the fall, she visited on weekends when she wasn't in school. By February she was pregnant, and they married in May.

For my father, this abrupt entry into family life meant the end of languid summers, fair-haired camp counselors, and getting by on next to nothing. He said later he worried about being able to support his family, that back then he had never really thought of marriage because of the financial burden, and his firm belief that adulthood was highly overrated. When he told me this over dinner when he was seventy-four, at first I thought, He should've gone with his hunch. The adulthood he never mastered; and as it turns out he never really made the leap from inheritance-subsidized bachelorhood to a providing family man. He was a coupon-clipping, stamp-recycling, food-hoarding, allowance-withholding fiend. Every time he spent money on us (even for medicine and food) it was as if he were grafting skin.

Though he was deeply in love with his teenaged girlfriend (my mother was fifteen and he was thirty-two—developmentally, I figure, they were peers), he had not yet translated his passion for her into any formal moves. The pregnancy forced his plans; and I am glad for that.

4

My brother and I spent long placid summers in the country with our grandparents in a house surrounded by fields of new, sweet hay. We fished for hornpout in the dark at Canterbury Pond in the quiet company of our grandfather, and took day trips with our Nana down the line to shop for new plastic toys and sugar-coated fruit candies (a treat our parents never would have allowed). When September came she would wring her apron in despair as she stood in the driveway while my brother and I climbed into our parents' '52 Chevy and rode off to our suburban home to begin another year of school.

My father, Sam, whose own mother was especially nonmaternal, basked in the exuberant attention and nurturance my mother's mother gladly offered. She loved my father because her daughter did; but also because she preferred men (they had the good sense to know what they needed—her; women, she knew, could provide for themselves); and because he charmed her. He consumed her food with zestful appreciation, took her doting with boyish gratitude, and they shared shallow gossip about townspeople they both knew. On summer nights in the country, she would chase him around her house, this bulky old woman, her eyes tearing from glee, and my lean, tanned father (seventeen years her junior) would dip in and out of door wells, closets, out onto the porch where his mother-in-law would corner him. She tickled him, the son she never had, until he recoiled into a pile of helpless laughter and pleas to stop, or until the supper began to burn. She fed him and hugged him. Both were deeply delighted to have each other in the family.

From September to late spring we lived in a roomy house with a pantry, secret stairs, and an attic filled with ancestors' gems. Our backyard had a blooming patch of jack-o'-lanterns, a flowering pear tree, and perfect places to hide. My brother and I and a dozen neighborhood kids played games in yards lit by the moon on autumn nights. I loved school (I got A's) and my friend Lorraine (she made me laugh and showed me how to use scalp-torturing hair rollers).

Early family life appealed to my father's playfulness. He would take out his old metal and wooden toys (one an intricate multicolored horse-racing set) and share them as if he were giving top secrets away. Then he would pack them up and put them away until the next unveiling. He said a song was named for us: "Sam and Janet Evening," and for years I didn't know the real song was "Some Enchanted Evening."

He was inventor and keeper of our family's customs. It was his way of imposing order on what he considered an otherwise absurd universe. He was an apolitical, non-tax-paying atheist who affected a gamesome rebellion against the conventions of adult life with farcical, often romantic ceremonies. When we went to the country every June, as soon as the car was parked, we followed our father on our short annual trek to the abandoned railroad station up the street to hunt for sweet fern. Finding the fern, and once inhaled, marked our rural initiation; then, intoxicated by summer's fragrance, we walked back behind our father to our grandparents' house to begin our seasonal stay.

My favorite ritual was when my father herded us out onto our unscreened front porch to witness thunderstorms. We sat brave, rained on, listening to the crackling drama in the sky, up close to our father in his rocker and we felt safe. What could have been a threatening weather condition—a dark violet and fiery sky—became a natural wonder in the company of my father, nothing to fret. He said later it was the best way he knew to make us unafraid of a storm, just as, years before, he had tried to take away my fear of the water by leading me to the slide.

My father told us often that he had what he wanted—two kids, one of each—perhaps because he knew and never forgot that he was not his parents' wish.

While my father created our family's ceremonies at home, he rarely accompanied us on our adventures outside of it. As a man of nearly forty, he had seen enough and had had his escapades. My mother, still in her early twenties when we were in grade school, delighted in showing her kids the world beyond, which she had hungered for and dreamed about as a stranded, precocious kid in her small rural town. She took us into the city at night and to all kinds of restaurants (the Casbah, Japanese, Italian). Because we had little money, my mother often shared soup or a big salad with us, and amiably ignored the slightly masked uppity annoyance of waiters who preferred not to bring three large spoons for one bowl, and liked even less the presence of children. We three sat entitled and grateful over our lemon-mint Mideastern salads and slurped unapologetically our egg drop soup in darkened alcoves with stiff linen napkins jutting out from under our chins.

She took us to abandoned houses at the beach (we climbed through them, illegally), cat shows, flower shows, concerts, and the airport—a view of possibilities, of planes, other kinds of people, places to go.

I can hear exactly the deep-felt cadence of her voice when she called me "love"; how much she meant it. I remember her devoted tutelage, whether when teaching me how to cut asparagus in the topaz light of a late summer afternoon in our yellow kitchen, just us, or when she introduced me to Guy de Maupassant in a small dark bookstore somewhere on Beacon Hill when I was not quite ten.

She was adamant about manners, she fought to get teachers who suited us (this was not popular in the 1950s), she made sure we knew books and art, and had lessons. She was the heart of the house, our passionate leader, so when she cracked, our family lost its balance.

The first sign of turbulence came in the winter of 1962, when I was eleven. My brother and I returned home from school to find our mother missing. We were not told where she went, but were instead jettisoned to the home of a neighbor. After two weeks of silent worry, we packed up our school clothes and blankets and headed back home.

When we returned, our mother seemed to be going further away by the day; and I felt my innocence being dragged away with her. I started to feel old quick. My father withdrew to his room, resentful of his breaking wife, and rarely emerged during daylight. As my friends became preoccupied with boys, dances, and makeup, I became distracted by my fading parent, and longed for adult-sized help.

My father was a Yankee jazz musician, my mother cultivated her own aristocratic (à la Oscar Wilde) sensibility—a rabid reaction to the rural underclass upbringing her adopted family provided—so my brother and I inherited a kind of Beat Puritanism. That meant you could refer, with a terse knowing wit, to other people's flawed minds, but not indulge speculation about one's own. And in the early sixties discussion about psyches was not common, and talk about sick psyches was especially touchy. Our family had lost its warm union and my mother became a shrill monarch who denied her sickness, so she refused to seek or receive treatment. In addition, our family had a high regard for self-containment, so therapy was not considered.

Eventually, my father took us awkwardly aside and told us that our mother had had a nervous breakdown. No details. Just that her mind wasn't right and she needed help. She was twenty-eight.

It seemed within a matter of days, my family pictures—of my winsome father who made us laugh, of my vibrant mother, of the four-of-us comfort—went blank.

5

My father was no patriarch, which was a large part of his appeal. On the rare occasions when he visited neighbors, I remember how slight he seemed in the company of other fathers. He was dwarfed by their gruffness. He sat delicately in his chair at the table in loafers and pastels with his long black hair swept back, and a clean gentle hand stretched over his crossed thigh. In white, short-sleeved shirts and short, organized hair, these guys strolled their kitchens in bulky dark shoes, hovering over my father as he sipped from a glass and they, the men, clutched bottles with callused hands. He relied on his humor and easy way with words to unite the bold differences between him and these head-of-household men. They found him puzzling, and were alternately awed by and resentful of his ability to pull off an escape from the usual demands of the gender.

Of course some of their bewilderment may have come from their sightings of him mowing the lawn in his boxer shorts. The front lawn, for God's sake. Sheer WASP obtuseness seemed to immunize him from the effects of neighborly tongue-wagging;

and it is likely that, if judgments were passed, they would have traveled swiftly past him, shielded as he was by his boyish eccentricity.

Sam seemed suspiciously unharnessed by and pleased with his lot—for a family man in the fifties. He made music on weekends—he had no nine-to-five job (aside from a brief attempt during which he was overcome by the incongruity of it all) or nagging wife, he took summers off, bowled and played tennis when he liked, and his young kids adored him. Our neighbors always seemed to view our lightheartedness with a wary eye; surely we were not as serious (or Christian) as a family ought to be.

The freedom my father took, he granted us. Just as he expected my mother, brother, and I would do what made us happy, never driving or nudging us in one direction or another, he assumed we were capable of our own defense.

My friend Lorraine recently said she was in awe of how respectfully my father treated his children.

"He spoke to you as if you were people," she said. "He seemed to think you could understand or handle just about anything. Like jazz, the stock market, his sophisticated kind of humor. He included you. He never talked down."

When I was twelve, I asked my father for money to buy art supplies for a card business I was launching. He agreed to sponsor my business, but only as a shareholder. He explained the meaning of net, profit, and overhead in the kitchen one night before bed, by writing notes on scrap pieces of paper which he suggested I file in the shoe box with my inventory of watercolors, ink, and pens.

My father never conferred on me a second-class importance, either as a kid or a girl. As someone who had a healthy disregard for conventional roles, he wasn't about to cultivate a girlish daughter. He took me to ball games (we talked stats), taught me how to bowl, liked that I was outgoing (as he would say), and expected my participation in all things. My brother and I shared all chores—except my brother probably did more dishes than I. I was regrettably sly about hiding food-encrusted pots in the freezer when it was my turn, which would mysteriously reappear when it was his. I cannot recall feeling confined by my father's expectations; on the contrary, my personhood was presumed.

Other postwar fathers who were afraid of their dreams mocked those of their sons or luckier men, while they, the providers, sat quietly desperate on their restless hands and made weekly money at work that left them yearning or with sore backs. The message in the fifties was that one ought to bury one's essential passion for the greater good of the family—sacrifice oneself for the larger unit. Fathers were expected to button down their visions and downsize their personal plans. When men familied, it was understood they would put away the paint sets, sell the motorcycles and saxophones, and do their duty. If they dared to indulge their private yens, they were considered selfish or immature, and there seemed to be no precedent for integrating dreams with work, art with responsibility. Thus, the conventional nuclear family was fueled by the slow secret simmer of deferred spirit. Mostly, the fifties manhood prototype didn't work. Duty alone does not feed the spirit; it was dishonest, impossible, and dreary. Yet as disinterested as he was in conforming, Sam never pursued, with committed ambition, the future in music I believe he could have had.

More than once, my father recalled the time he had sent a song he had written, when he was in his twenties, to a New York record producer who responded promptly and with enthusiasm. "He wanted me to go to the city and sell him on it; it was too complicated, I didn't want to get into the competitive show biz thing," he said, affecting a nonchalant dismissal of what he probably deemed his one shining, albeit deferred, invitation to the Big Time. He kept the producer's letter in a box of valuables until the day he died. But he never turned in his passion for the piano—he kept playing.

Sam came of age in the Rat Pack era, when guys hung out with guys against the rules, when women were chicks, men were cats, alcohol was booze, cool was hip, and a good Drambuie and a simple, clever lyric were as philosophical as it got. I remember noticing my father's transformation in the company of other jazz musicians—he became lively and elated by a sense of belonging; and he wanted us to go there too. He trained and quizzed my brother and me in jazz appreciation from the very beginning. When Ella Fitzgerald, Lena Horne, or Count Basie would come on the car radio, he would say, "Okay, who's this?" Once I answered Johnny Mattress when Mathis swooned over the airwaves, and my father smiled approvingly. He taught me the left-hand part of the boogie-woogie when I was eight.

He and the trumpet and trombone players and the drummer (we called them uncles) came late at night, were there in the mornings, sometimes for supper and on weekends. They fancied themselves a creative, carousing bunch on the run from the constraints of family life. Except for the trombone player, who was the eternal bachelor when unmarried men were chic; we heard about the ladies he dated and he winked at us kids a lot. (My mother, then still in her early twenties, seemed pleased to be included in their company.) The trumpet player, whose upper lip had been flattened and made shiny by many years of horn blowing, sang scat and drew intense, charcoal sketches of musicians in smoky clubs. His wife had a glossy blond chignon. Sam was the reasonable band member, inflammable, never drunk, no smoker, quick-witted, easy. On one of these occasions, I remember Sam punning off-colorfully that Sinatra's flamboyantly confident tune, "I've Got the World on a String," was the theme song for Tampax.

I felt a tiny bit scared and hugely impressed with their worldliness—they traded jokes I never got (though they were more than willing to include a kid in the good time), and then would erupt in wild manly laughter. The room was alive and they were on. They casually jiggled ice in short glasses half full of amber liquor, spoke jazzese and appreciatively of uninhibited broads who could run with the pack, and seemed to be having more fun than I could imagine an adult ever having. They were classy, and, at all costs, unserious—an exhilarating contrast to the temperate churchgoing folks in my neighborhood, for whom Friday night grocery shopping at the new, brightly lit Stop & Shop was a semiformal event. My father had found in his sphere of music a home where he fit and felt loose.

He admired Erroll Garner, a jazz musician with whom he shared an ability to play the piano by ear. My father's left hand would pound a back beat, sometimes with dragging strokes, while the right hand scrambled up and down and across the keys, with quick plunks, and smart, quirky timing. Like Garner, Sam became entranced when he played, erotically coaching the notes with elfin grunts. He was so intimately entwined with his music, the listener felt both seduced and voyeuristic. And touched by the uncharacteristic depth he seemed to achieve and the emotion he dared to summon in the creation of his music.

After supper, when I was young, my father would often amble into the den, sit at the piano, and play for my mother. She would tuck her legs under her, drape her arm over the back of a chair, look into his face, then lean her head back and listen. She became so enthralled with her husband's music, she seemed to fall in love with him all over again each time. We kids were told not to interrupt, so we stayed away, sensing from other rooms that our parents were intimately lost in each other. When he finished, he'd break into a smile, vulnerable and at rest. I do believe for him his music became, maybe always was, a preferred place. Real life was anti-jazz.

When as an adult I went to hear him play in bands in the city, I was struck, rendered teary often, by how generous and confident an accompanist he was. He gave quietly, fully, exquisitely to his fellow jazzists from his shadowed perch at the piano.

I feel lucky to have been allowed in, if only marginally and briefly, to the playful province my father held so dear. (The guys stopped coming around when Sam's marriage soured.) Even now, in my middle age, I can't seem to get enough of Sinatra; I'm drawn to the late fifties cocktail culture—the sophisticated, cavalier innocence of an era which would be sneered at in the current decade's climate of correctness. My father and some of his friends were not model family men—their contagious jazz aura captured them so completely that, interpersonally, they had little left to give, and next to no interest in giving it; their most flattering roles were as performers, uncles, playboys, and pals. But, before their time, they were a motley and equitable group (my father started one of the first integrated jazz bands in the Boston area). It was simple: if you could keep up, you could come on board, but you had to *love* the music.

I am increasingly grateful that I was able to see up close an elegant kind of fun that has all but vanished. I love the sauciness of "That's Why the Lady Is a Tramp" (sung without derision), the rousing, inviting lyrics ("Come fly with me, come fly, come fly a-way . . ."), the giddy banter on one of my tapes between Sinatra and a (seemingly) drunken Dean Martin, the 1959 movie *A Hole in the Head* (which I first saw with my father when I was eight) about a money-squandering, chick-chasing hotel owner (Sinatra) but devoted, in his way, single father.

Sometimes I would think: Should a man who makes music

like this be expected to do anything else? Shouldn't we, his family, have freed him from all other obligations, so he could fly and we, on the lucky occasion, could soar with him?

For years I wondered to what degree and at what cost we should subsidize the artful expressions of others. Should those of us for whom coping comes more easily simply sweep up and shut up? Surely Leonardo da Vinci, Monet, and Dylan Thomas hired housekeepers, accountants, or had supportive wives (the suffering wind beneath their wildly flapping creative wings?). But at what expense do the wives and families provide the wind? As I get older and nearer my art, I get closer to what I think is just: that we should all learn to provide our own aerodynamics, jazz makers among them, and then help to make sense of life's regular trials, so we all have a chance to fly.

But I am glad my father cared enough, when he did, to want to share the place where he kept his spirit. Revisiting the music has brought an uncommon comfort; and my father would be pleased my taste for his music has endured and grown. Of course, if Sam knew that George Jones's twangy ballads gave me chills, he'd be groaning in his hereafter. Then again, he might just utter, with circumspect restraint, "Hmmmm . . . eclectic."

Left to reside in a home without shelter and in a family without parents, I was hurried out of my youth into a state of diligence and caution. I began to feel as if it were my job to keep very close touch with reality, because my mother couldn't and my father wouldn't. At the age of eleven, before my first kiss and just after I lost interest in dolls, I began my vigil. I would think straight enough for us all.

For days, weeks, years, then decades, I waited for my mother's return, for her to rebound in a glow of maternal love and remorse for the lost time and the terrifying insanity—and for my father to find my mother beautifully young and lovable again, for him to start smiling, for us to be a family again. I wanted him to come out of his room, open the shades and let the sun in, clean up the mess, round up his children, march into the center of the house, and take charge.

But it never happened. Sam was not a complicated man; he met conflict with a confounded, tizzied resentment. Whatever surge of energy he experienced during our varying degrees of crisis, he employed not in resolving the problem but in wishing it away. And of course the problem never went very far.

The more difficult life became, the more my father sought refuge in the periphery. His wife did not clean or cook; she made messes and left them. My father withheld money and food, distanced himself from my mother, and became embittered by her refusal to participate, even minimally, in our family.

Eventually he resented the family that filled his house. As my brother and I got bigger, smarter, and separate, and his teenage bride grew up and more complex, my father staked out his own territory, claiming no-trespassing spaces within his house— he had his chair, his ice cream, his towel, his glass. I've observed this in other men; once a love affair turns into a family, some men do not know how to share the space without getting lost in the uncertain swirl of familial motion. When his lover becomes a mother, a man's previously exclusive relationship becomes inclusive. Merging feels threatening, and multiple dynamics overwhelm; so some men make locks and mark routes within the family home.

Women, as bearers of children and homemakers, have not

only had to be engaged in simultaneous activities, but they begin their maternal lives by providing residency for their children within their very bodies, which often continue to nourish them for months after. For a woman, private domain hardly seems an issue when it is literally impossible, in the beginning, to tell where her body ends and her child's begins. When the kids actually appear and begin to share the house, a mother can be grateful to sit alone, let alone to claim a chair.

Emergencies, in particular, sent my father into exile. He was not fired into action but rather swamped by the weight. Playing he could do. He dutifully met the compromises required of him in a moderately functioning family—food shopping, diaper changing, school registration, providing money for holiday gifts. But he turned away from the hard work.

Anything that did not present itself as an agent of immediate pleasure or personal significance my father labeled foolish or discarded at once. In his refuse pile fell: religion, politics, income taxes, marriage, intimacy, war, bras (comparable, he said, to wearing a jockstrap full time), and flavored coffee ("redundant"). That which held his interest included food (especially fresh corn and soft-centered chocolates), baseball on the radio, the scent of sweet fern, Julie Christie, and jazz.

He could not seem to be able to go far beyond the comfort of the moment; or past the age of eighteen, which appeared to be the terminus of his emotional growth (the year his mother died).

Expecting my father to shore up the disaster of our tumbling matriarchy would've been like asking the Queen Mother to clean the commode; or expecting Peter Pan to play tight end. Much of the world was too abrasive, and our wrecked family, in particular, was painfully puzzling to this innocent man.

As an only child, and the only male in a broad tier of

female cousins, he was adored and relied on for his charm and mild masculine manner. He was the eternal invitee, the celebrated boy, always welcome in the company of friends and at family gatherings. He played tennis, attended college, was polite, and had a quick, inoffensive wit—all resources readily redeemable within his privileged class; and fully transferable to his world of jazz. Stepping out of his illustrious youth, albeit unfulfilled for the most part at home, was a displeasing transition for him. It was icky; he would have, like Bartleby the Scrivener, preferred not to.

When our family fell, he possessed no impulse to fight for or protect anyone. But then he never had seen the sense in extreme conviction—not for the sake of his sick wife, the freedom of his country, not for his kids, and certainly not to defend a manhood he was not entirely convinced he wanted.

No one, it seemed, had ever protected him. Both his socially conscious mother and her deferential husband lived for outings and status, making it all too clear to their son that he could be either a hindrance or an asset to their chosen lifestyle, but never an entity in his own right. When his mother died in a car accident, his father, with whom he was living, could not find the courage to identify his wife at the morgue. He sent his son instead. After her death, my father's father quit his job as an executive with a lock company and stopped talking. He hoarded his grief and retreated from his only child, who may have needed comfort at the time of his mother's death. Like his father before him who could not carry on, my father, too, could not face down the loss of my mother's mind and attend his family.

In an intact environment, within the steady presence of another parent, it is possible Sam could have remained a supporting yet vital player. We could have tolerated, protected, even, his oddities, both annoying and endearing; we could have continued to go to him for fun and play, for his brief but earnest tutorials in money management. Just as my mother could have stayed viably crazy within the warm refuge of a husband's resilient devotion and hardy passion. Even when she was ill, my mother remained sensual and fragile, vulnerable to pleasure, and my father, it was always clear, was her favorite lover. She never lost her ardent attraction to him; though he (owing, it seemed, to an abbreviated attention span in matters of intimacy and romance) had lost interest in his marriage even before she crashed, a rejection she found unbearable.

I wish he had taken her to the dark quiet of his room, whispered her into calmness, stroked her hair until the torturous noise inside was silenced. He could have nursed her through the bad patches, hugged her through the pain and isolation, taken her side against her imagined persecutors. "I can see how you'd be angry, Sara," he could've said when she complained of the consuming conspiracies she imagined. He could've accepted his wife as a woman with an illness that demanded Promethean patience if he could've kept the reasons he had loved her to begin with. Instead, he confirmed her worst dread by abandoning her, making her feel unlovable when she slipped from sanity. He would fume in disgust, personalizing her sickness, and walk away. He had not gotten enough love himself, and he didn't have the insight to know he might find it by giving. So they deserted each other, bequeathing loneliness in larger doses than either of them had ever known or ever could have imagined.

When the walls and floors fell away, there was nothing and no one to contain my father; he inherited impossibly high orders—to stay the course—and he could not do it. In the midst of his wife's fast-forward demolition, my father ducked for cover, leaving his kids on the front lines to fend for themselves against our mother's belligerent illness.

He took to his room for the solitude he needed to refuel his charm, his best asset, settled into his sagging womb of a mat-

tress, read, and listened to the radio. The drama of illness and
anger, of which he perceived himself the beleaguered target (but
of which he was in part the source), justified an already committed lack of giving. When he was at home, he spent nearly all of
the last few years of our family life prone, wrapped in his protective, threadbare blankets.

My father's painstaking fumbling during our family's most
desperate days disproves the axiom that God gives us what we
can handle. This divine plan, this dogged family drama in which
he found himself inextricably cast, was clearly meant for a different address, another man.

7

Until recently, when I saw a father with his child, I used to be
stunned into a degrading silence. It did not matter whether the
father was happily engaged or distant and coarse. A father's presence was a glittering blip that amplified the tragic absence of him
everywhere else. A withdrawn father evoked rage for the work
I've had to do because he didn't—with my kids, for the kid I was.
I tried to talk myself through it. I applied all my internal remedies, but I could not be tranquilized, I could not get out from
under it. For me, witnessing father love, in all its forms, brought
on a tsunami of sorrow and envy—brief but undeniable despair
for the loss of authority, protection, and rescue that a father
could bring, for the man at the end of the slide who would catch
me.

And when I heard the word "Dad," I dissolved for the
moment into a heap of longing—not just for me but for my kids,
my brother, for the men I've loved who missed the fathers they

had, for the thousands of kids who'll never say the word. I did not call my father Dad for the last thirty years of his life, and I rarely hear my kids say it. The want in the word is heart-stopping. The hope it beckons . . . It is the same kind of sorrowful joy I feel at weddings when two people stare down the prickly odds and declare for all the world their brave and significant dreams—that they will love each other through it all until the end.

Dad. It is a vow against all odds, in the face of countless examples to the contrary. Dad. It does not have the utilitarian effect of Mum or Ma. It's still spoken as a ballad refrain. It's a pledge that originates in the heart and fights for life amid the carnage of persistent, obvious history to the contrary and excruciatingly scant follow-through. Mother love is aplenty and apparent: we complain because we have too much of it. The love of a father is an uncommon gem, to be hunted, burnished, and hoarded. The value goes up because of its scarcity.

The kind of father I ached for I have never seen, except in glimpses I have embellished with wishful imaginings. Does my version of fatherhood exist? I wonder. Can a man be affectionate and responsible, tender and organized, firm and flexible? Can a father have an authority which emanates from selfless love? Have the good fathers among us been so called because we imply a "compared to . . ."? Maybe. But the fathering I missed may never have been, and perhaps has yet to be invented.

Again and again, the word fails to keep the promise of a loving kinship we sit on the edge of our collective seats and root for, hope for, coax into being. It is a reminder simply of what could've been but wasn't—a life raft denied.

It is unfair to expect (and impossible to find) a fatherly or motherly love to come from anyone besides our parents; though the unreserved love of friends and lovers is the salve we need. Sometimes men and women behave in their couplehoods like children looking to get and failing to find the denied ingredients of their respective childhoods—we unconsciously crave the protection or acceptance we didn't get enough of, then blame and resent our partners because they will not and cannot provide it. Or we seek what we knew, replay the familiar, and resent them even more.

Having grown up, now at a reasonable distance from and many years away from the man I knew and loved first, I realize it is not so much the father I write about here, but the daughter he left behind. He had a story, with a history that hurt him too. It's just that some of his shortcomings happened to fall squarely and heavily on me.

But I have never wished for a different father. Sam felt deeply familiar to me, and I felt positively, consistently indigenous among the members of my family. We shared humor, seasons, intimate rituals, and references both personal and social—what my mother referred to as our mutual "mental geography." As a kid, and for many years after, I never felt, as some of my friends often did and still do of their families: Who are these people; and how did I get here? I never wanted anyone else's family or father. I wanted mine, only more.

The older I get and the more women I meet whose fathers reduced their girls' dreams to fit ladylike ambition; whose fathers were cruel or autocratic, superior or fawning to a fault, the luckier I feel. I emerged into the world believing I had all of what I needed to do what I wanted, a result, I am convinced, not only of my mother's commitment to raise a self-confident daughter but of my father's comfort with the range of my expressed ambition, whether it was my bodacious card business, acting in plays, or wanting to learn how to catch a hard ball without flinching. The management of money was important for me to know, as he presumed one day I would be making my own.

Back then my upbringing did not mirror that of girls whose fathers seemed to shield their delicate girls from the antics of boys and the harsh complexities of a "man's world"; my father's relaxed backstage manner, the absence of his overpowering and perceptible doubt, gave me the sure message of his faith in me. What he gave, finally, is what he failed to proffer—a controlling claim on my unique self, or a mocking dismissal of a girl's head-strong plans. He did not come to the fore when we needed a savior, because he had abandoned the throne long ago.

My father gave me a fear of the free fall but, ultimately, the self-reliance to navigate it.

8

The closest my father and I came to true affinity was during the early hours of a Saturday morning, about 3 A.M., when I was fourteen. A drunken mistress, hell-bent on finding my father, had awakened us all by pounding on our front door, calling his name and damning her lover. Semi-asleep and startled, we all emerged from our respective rooms. My mother, already launched in her plans to separate from her husband, yelled to my brother to get the camera (divorce evidence). For my mother, worn from years of emotional adultery and ill more than well, this fiasco was oppressively anticlimactic, trivial almost.

I stood at the top of the stairs looking down, eventually letting the woman in. She was long and slender, and was holding her slingback Papagallos in one hand and a whiskey tumbler in the other, the contents of which had dribbled down the front of her dark sheath. Her bouffant was deflated and dangling; she looked like Anne Sexton on a binge—a wayward blueblood, adrift in drink and a sea of abandoned decorum; she awkwardly, painfully proclaimed her desire for my father. (It is not easy watching a well-heeled woman so utterly out of her station.) I told her he was in his room and would not come out, and then somewhat protectively suggested she leave before a really bad scene erupted. On my way back upstairs, I remember thinking: My father must be a nut magnet. What's the deal with him and cuckoo women? This was a bad suburban comedy.

We convened in the narrow hallway outside of my father's room, imploring him to come out. Eventually, he unlocked his door and passed through the knot of his fuming family on his way to coaxing his distressed lover out of our house. As he passed me, he caught my eye and mumbled, in a moment of acute perception: "I guess I'm kind of like New York City. A good place to visit but you wouldn't want to live there." I always loved him for that line.

On that busy, disastrous night, he was exasperated and embarrassed enough to admit his regret for the inadequacies that were him. Eavesdropping, we three waited silently upstairs as my father made promises that pleased his lover and eventually persuaded her to leave. My brother and I looked at each other before returning to our rooms. My mother shook her head and closed her door.

Self-awareness in a man goes a long way with me. An ounce of reflection is worth its weight in gold. It's an invitation to understanding—to a meeting place of close, momentary accord. Much can be forgiven, even, almost, a father's bumbling infidelity, if he makes an effort to see himself and be truly seen by others.

9

I had visited my father's house on only a few occasions during the years between the divorce and his death. When our family split up, my mother never considered keeping the house, it belonged so thoroughly to her husband. She wanted out and I went with her to an apartment in the city and my brother moved in with our grandparents in the country. When I visited as an adult, my childhood home always felt smaller and browner than I had remembered it, as if the walls and lights had been cast in coffee stains and been yellowed by years of cigarette fumes. When I went upstairs, touring the paths of a house I had once known so well, I stepped lightly, feeling as though I might disrupt the surroundings my father had so deliberately reclaimed.

The house that had once been filled with my mother's kitchen aromas, vivid embroideries, and scattered stacks of partially devoured books, but which had been finally marked by the spoor of her madness, had been shanghaied by the man left behind. He had cleared out signs of family and ambivalence, and had transformed the home that had been ours into a desolate bunker—with stiff, gray secondhand furniture, empty surfaces, and small precise piles of stamps and coupons in the corners of the buffet. His kitchen was tidy and deserted—the half-dozen wide yellow shelves in the pantry left gaping and hardly necessary for one man's supply of cheese sauce and tuna—three cans to be exact. Mostly, there were no smells; the cool temperature he maintained (a heat-saving habit) had neutralized the scent of lives being lived.

Our house had had the heart knocked out of it, was now weary and, it seemed, had lost its nerve to be a home again.

In my mother's empty bedroom Sam had stored a decade's worth of *Time* magazines—he liked his news brief and weekly—in dozens of tall, neat stacks up against and obscuring the impressionistic pastel wallpaper my mother had defiantly bought and put up after years of living with what had been her husband's mother's dingy thirty-year-old selection. He had replaced the memory of his wife's ephemeral, damaged presence with summarized data, seizing the space with aggressive order.

It had been a beautiful room, in the corner of the house, with a high half window made of rose and amber glass, and light oak floors. My mother had taken down the dark green shades years before and had left the windows bare, open to the light; which made the neighbors and my father slightly uneasy. It is the room I raced into after school, to sprawl across the foot of her bed and tell her my day; the room I wandered into to find her sleepy, warm body when I felt sick at night and where I saw her undress in the deep, sweet-smelling closet, the curve of her breasts and pale soft figure half hidden behind hanging shirts.

Sam's room had grown darker, more womblike; it had aged as if abandoned, the dusty, large oval-framed photos of his parents still on the wall above his headboard, his mattress sinking closer to the floor, the shades still drawn. His room had become more of an enclosure than a bedroom over the years, a shadowy place in which he could be free of bother and blind to the light of day.

But when I visited, we never talked, not about our family's fall, our estrangement, his failure to send child support or the college tuitions my brother and I earned and were granted by holding multiple jobs and keeping high grades. Then, in his house that had been ours, revisiting our collapsed history would've been unbearable; to sit in the chairs in the rooms where the drama had unfolded, in slow, agonizing spasms, would've stung too much.

Now, in my house, before it was too late, during his visit about a year before he died, I wanted my say; and his old age revealed a vulnerability that suggested he might want to have his say too. He was sitting up on his bed in the guest room of my house, when I knocked on the door and said I wanted to talk. The instant I spoke, the words seemed wearily gratuitous, mean almost, though I did not feel vengeful and had long ago passed the blame. I sought, I think, a brief acknowledgment, maybe an apology, from the man who was my father, or a chance, perhaps, for him to offer an insight which could soothe the bitter letdown of years ago.

I told him that for most of our life together he was not what I thought a father ought to be. Not that I knew what a father should be, but with children of my own I knew I was doing lots of work he had never done. "You failed to support or protect us. You withheld money and food," I said, "when we needed at least that." I told him that my brother and I never should've had to handle the divorce (we had consulted with the lawyer when our parents didn't or wouldn't). And he seemed to blame my mother for her illness. "You must know she could not help it," I said.

He said he thought he did the right thing. He got a job, even, and said he intended to stay married but she wanted out. He said he felt isolated, like the enemy, in the years before the divorce, and that he didn't know what to do. I know he didn't.

It did not matter that I was speaking my truth. It was too late in the day . . . he sat on the bed listening, blind, puzzled, feeling wrong for reasons he could not grasp, or was too far from now to summon.

I know he had been rocked by the revelations of our talk. And though, in his tender, waning state, I sensed he ached for help in scaring away his loneliness, he had lived too long in his innocence to break through now.

On his way to the car the next day, as I guided him out of the door, my father, never an affectionate man, brought his face close to mine for a kiss and whispered, "I still love you. Is that okay?"

10

For my father to have endured his final days, months, years in medicine land, in the company of other waning humans, would have been a vicious penance he did not deserve. He subscribed to the faux Christian Science approach: this-too-shall-pass common sense, no pills, no cost, lots of water and rest.

Eight days after his stroke, with faint visible progress, an obvious unwillingness to endure physical therapy, and the emotional affirmation of the hospital's psychiatrist of my father's unambivalent wish to die, the hospital released him to our care. We had fought hard for him; and during the last week of his life, at home in my brother's house, he showed a resolve none of us had seen while he had been living. He did not want to live; and in the hospital he had used all of what he had—an attempted body lunge, sounds forced from his throat, disconnecting his feeding tube, pulling away from medication—to say this and stand firm. When he was home, he lay still, unresponsive and stoic, bearing the discomfort of malnutrition and dehydration and bravely staring down the fright of death itself, following through with unimaginable courage.

The night my father died David and I drove to Boston, went into the house where my brother and his family, and a hospice worker, shuffled through his apartment, quietly exchanging information. He had made plans, in keeping with his contempt for waste, to donate his body to Harvard Medical and wanted no memorials.

I wanted to see my father. My brother followed me into the room where he lay dead, and we stood on either side of him—and said nothing for several minutes. I looked at his face, a bleached papier-mâché mask arched up toward the ceiling—frozen by a final gasp—and grieved for the man whose single ambition was to take himself to the century mark as comfortably as possible. Dead at seventy-five, he did not even reach what he would've called a ripe old age. He lay defeated, moderately old, disqualified, not even a runner-up in his only personal contest. In the end even his well-cared-for body failed him.

But why did he want to live so long? Surely not because he had unmet obligations, ambitions to realize, plans to finish? Did he think longevity would dissolve all his fears? Did he think, by living gently, he could charm even the Grim Reaper into turning back? (Charm is not bad. But without the will or the gut to go deeper, it leaves everyone feeling slightly lonely.) Maybe he thought that if he lived long enough Death might lose interest and go away altogether, or *he* would, and would mind less this final imposition.

Maybe his plan to live long was his consuming hymn against the uncompromising event of adulthood, which, I believe, was his ulterior dread. Just as he put off family and work until his thirties when an unplanned pregnancy decided for him, he had hoped for a long life that could buy him time in which to conjure up some semblance of the cherished childhood he never had and kept thinking he might get (from mothering lovers, though his final affair was a costly enmeshment with a zealously maternal woman), but which finally eluded him. When my parents divorced, my father asked plaintively: "Who will take care of me?" And then assumed my grandmother (my mother's mother) would fill in. He could not be a man or a father while he was still waiting for his mother's embrace.

And maybe he kept thinking, as soon as the weight of adulthood passed, he could welcome back his guileless youth, though he never seemed to be able to clean up enough to make the resurrection possible.

But by the time he had reached his seventy-fourth year he wanted out—to be released from the colorless version of life brought on by his blindness and dependence; it had gone on long enough. He had said several times, while I walked and he staggered next to me, his arm in mine, that not being able to see had taken away "about ninety-five percent of life worth living." In a more ambitious man, having no sight could've sparked a challenge, at least, to invent other ways to see, to discover books on tape, Braille, to meet and know other blind people, to refine his other instincts. My father saw it as more of the same, another onslaught to be tolerated and wished away. He stumbled through each day, making do, wired to his radio by earphones, waiting for someone to make it better, and becoming embittered because no one did.

During the last year he was alive, we met for dinner every other week, and occasionally he would pull out his wallet with uncomfortable but determined magnanimity and ask me to identify the bills he would use to pay for our meal. And together we reviewed his life.

"You have to admit," he said, "earning your way through college gave you character, self-reliance." It did, I said. "You've done well," he proclaimed, taking comfort in offering himself the reprieve that comes with a you-can't-quarrel-with-the-results rationale. He wanted to remember his early summers in the country, his jazz friends, and for me to help recall our family stories.

One night before our meals arrived, he asked about my mother, wistfully, whom he had not seen in over twenty years. We half-seriously flirted with the idea of her visiting him. He admitted to being lonely and missing the touch of a woman. "She knows I'm blind, does she?" She did and, I added light-heartedly, she had become slightly self-conscious about being a few pounds overweight, and maybe wouldn't mind not being seen.

"One thing about her, she was sexy." He liked that about her from the start, he said. I told him that during one of the few visits I had had with her in the last several years she had asked about him too. He beamed distantly. "Hmmm, wouldn't that be something," he murmured with irony, seeming to dream up a reunion that would take place in a future he couldn't know he didn't have. Two weeks later he was dead.

A month after my father died I met with my mother, and over coffee we held a private, emotional memorial to the man we had loved and lost. We remembered my father's humor and his willingness to change diapers "long before that was fashionable"; and her husband's acceptance of his nonconforming wife, how in the early years he tolerated her aversion to housework, and—he the keeper of tightly hoarded savings—bought a dishwasher instead. She recalled sorrowfully the divorce. "Just when we could have had each other, you kids were getting older. He was an easy man to live with, I could've . . ."

She said she was furious with him for retreating but, in between choking back tears, that she never stopped loving him, and I knew she hadn't. "I would've liked to have seen him," she said when I told her that he had mentioned wanting to see her. And then I cried too, both relieved and pained by having realized the secret dream a child of divorced parents never quite gives up; that my father and mother had never loved anyone as deeply or as enduringly as they had loved one another. That in the end, both lonely and worn out, with nothing left to tell but the truth, they could reveal a desire that had outlasted their hapless decades apart; that with time they might've known and maybe loved each other again.

11

My father died, leaving my brother and me all of his tightly hoarded savings and the remainder of his blue chip stocks (he had sold most of them over the years to meet expenses). All of our withheld allowances, the quarters he fined us for not brushing our teeth or for forgetting chores, the college tuitions he never paid, the child support he failed to send, the food money he wouldn't share—all of it came tumbling back, a time-released return of our childhood cache. In the year before he died, when his ex-girlfriend contested her share of an account in both their names, he was adamant about us having it all, venturing, even, into the courts after having avoided all manner of legal formality his whole life (including the payment of income taxes, which my brother and I remedied after his death). He wanted to be assured that his kids would have his money; and within months after his death, the judge ruled in our favor. He fought on our behalf as a father, as if the dedicated fight, *despite the discomfort,* was to be his final bequest to his children.

For me, it seemed somehow harder to lose a father I had barely had than it would've been to have lost a man I had known who had fathered us thoroughly and well.

I know I am not alone in the behemoth voyage to "understanding father." It is an expedition uniquely arduous, because our men have left so few traces behind. We knew our mothers better; they revealed more, if only in their interactions with us, their kids. To find our fathers, the men we barely knew, we set out, with imprecise maps and a dearth of clues, to find the souls *they* barely knew they had, hoping, in the search, to find the unfinished part of ourselves. Our fathers have been remiss; they have exited with their undisclosed intentions, leaving behind only cold puzzles whose resolutions we, their successors, are hungry to imagine.

All the brutally squandered years, the damned waste of a teasing closeness that came only with the smell of death. My father went to his grave (or the medical lab as the case was) leaving a hint of what life could've been had he reached and been reachable long ago. Why does it take the heavy-breathing moan of mortality to call to the fore what really matters? He departed, poised at the gateway with a dawning appetite for intimacy, after a lifetime of not being known, without trading joys, hurts, or fears with those he loved. And that is the deepest regret of his death.

In the weeks after my father died, my brother and I went through his possessions: his canvas Boston Marathon entry number, a small box of jewelry containing presumably his mother's wedding and engagement rings, old yearbooks, letters from sweethearts. But most prominent in his collected belongings were boxes full of jazz—notes, clippings, fliers, cards, photos, the letter from the New York music producer, and dozens of old 78rpm records. I knew he loved his music, but when I found his obviously treasured inventory, I felt as if I had gone into a child's closet only to discover beloved but dangerous toys he had prom-

ised to stop playing with. I wished immediately that I had somehow recognized more his consuming tie to his music; or realized
how much he defined himself by his gift to play.

There were photographs, mostly of his parents and girl
cousins, and many that revealed a man different than the father I
had known. He is tanned, lean, shirtless in loose pleated pants
near the stone wall in Barnstead where he had begun a ceremonial rock pile in his teens and which we added to every summer
when our family was young. Or he is nattily suited up, in blazers
and bucks, or tennis whites (for all of his life with us he was a
parody of fashion apathy), in the country for the day, posing with
big-bosomed aunts in wide flowery hats and stern-looking mus-
tachioed uncles in derbies and tight jackets in front of shiny
black late-model cars.

He's on a Florida beach in the fifties, his head resting on
the bathing-suited bellies of happy women, or playing the piano
in dim-lit bars. His green eyes are sparkling, his smile is broad
and easy, his straight black hair is clipped into flattering angles
above his broad, smooth forehead. In many of the pictures he
was—well, there's no other word for it—frolicking. Giddy and
liberated, handsome, very, very handsome. Life before the del-
uge. And I think for a minute, but only for a minute, it is where
he should have stayed—on the beach, with lucid, sexy lovers, at
the piano, keeping it simple.

Looking at the man in the pictures, I see a guy who pulled
himself away from a good time to face down the seriousness of
adulthood and family life. Which I am convinced he truly loved,
if briefly, if ambivalently, if not enough or as passionately as he
loved jazz, and his slow, summer youth.

Part 2
Brother

you were my genius, you
my cast-iron Viking . . .
Years later now you're young

your breast open, your belt dragged down
by an old-fashioned thing, a sword
the last bravado you won't give over
though it weighs you down as you stride.

—ADRIENNE RICH
Orion, a poem

1

Of my brother and me, it would have to have been said that when we were young I was the more macho. There is a photo of us when we are about four and five in the backyard of our house on an autumn afternoon. My brother is crouched in the tall grass with a floral babushka tied on his head, from which straight sprouts of close-cropped fair hair are escaping. His pointer finger is pressed over pursed lips. He is deep in contemplation, with heavy lids and long lashes flapped over his protruding blue eyes. I am bent over him, my small fleshy fingers sprawled over firmly bent knees, giving counsel to my older (by ten months) brother. I am the bossy manager, and my brother in glamorous drag is contentedly cooperative in this picture, undaunted by his secondary but clearly honored role and cross-gender affect.

When we were older, and my brother's best friend visited, he would quote from Dylan in dry asides when he observed the force of my girlish confidence. "The sun's not yellow, it's chicken," he'd snicker, suggesting I did not suffer fools, much less fiery planets, kindly. I was not coy. No one had suggested I should be.

My brother was genteel by the age of three, a born WASP,

my mother would say, and seemed to be quietly busy within a slow-moving internal world. By the age of seven, he would often sit silent for hours in thrall to a new book. He was so careful with his allowances and paper route income (he saved his money in a glass jar in the top right-hand drawer of his organized desk) that my mother and I negotiated loans from him when he was barely nine (my father was a tougher benefactor). And he never complained when I lapsed into what my mother referred to as my Ethel Merman phase. I was often gratuitously loudmouthed in an otherwise low-toned family.

Back then I used to feel (and still do) that being a girl seemed a much broader experience than being a boy. Girls could move more easily, with less to prove; they were welcome to remain in the comfort of home. Boys were sent out into the unpredictable world of other boys, armed with expectations to compete with, dare, or conquer the opposition (other boys). I could still play cowboys and Indians and go happily home without feeling my gender was in question when I lost the standoff.

As my brother got older I witnessed, through the eyes of an adoring, sheltering sister, the attempted genderfication of a boy. I saw him awkwardly, haltingly try to measure up to what I was sure was an inferior act, all the while not wanting to lose him to the prevailing myopia of maleness. Clay did not seem to have the armor he needed for the abrasive induction into a gender which was at once alien and insulting. My father was not inclined to impose boy standards (he had pulled off a wily escape of his own out of the ranks of conventional masculinity); and my mother was conflicted.

As a growing girl I did not feel as if I had to behave in any prescribed way; that I could just exist and continue to be, free of any kind of standard of performance. But my brother faced a series of explicit, emphatic breaks, that would turn him away from his mother, out into the world of other males. I did not need to go anywhere to learn about my femaleness, my mother embodied my destination. My brother was sent forth to differentiate, even though his nature was more aligned with hers than my own.

I remember my mother, as if responding to an enforced social order that clashed terribly with her own instincts, systematically clipping her tender ties with her son. Like the fall morning she refused my eight-year-old brother's kiss at the door before we left for school; it was time, she said, for that kind of affection to stop. My brother obliged and turned away from the person he loved the most. And throughout his school years she made sure he had male teachers, even though his most inspired teacher, the one who watched over him with full-hearted concern, was a woman. My mother believed she was giving my brother what he should have. She was aware of her parental mandate to socialize the boy, but she was committed to sheltering his spirit too. She said many years later that she never resolved it.

Clay and I grew up happily parallel, relying on each other, playing at the same pace, often in the same places among common friends. Watching Clay so closely in the earliest years left me with a wholehearted compassion for boys. I have always been moved by the innocence of unwitting pre-men, who guilelessly graze the pasture before the torturous branding.

I remember exactly when I became seized by empathy. My brother and I attended a one-room schoolhouse, where the first and second grades shared a large open room. I sat in the first-grade row closest to Mrs. Horner's second-grade class as my brother's sentinel, having mastered a discreet peripheral glance while seeming to pay attention to Mrs. Shields while she walked us through phonics. On the other side of the room, reading groups of varying abilities formed small chatty circles, and then there was my brother, often a group of one, isolated for his puzzling inability to translate the words—diagnosed in the third grade, finally, as dyslexia. He was quiet and often distracted. I wanted to take his place in his singled-out seat, answer the questions he couldn't, and fought a simmering ache every time I saw or thought I saw him struggle. Years later my brother said he wasn't anywhere near the fragile kid I thought he was; he was simply living in his head, dreamily distant from the dull activity around him.

As we got older I guarded him still, albeit silently, especially when his boyhood was on the line. My sibling symbiosis sharpened my view from his eyes, boy eyes. When we went to school dances together, as adolescents, I watched girls make fun of boys who asked them to dance. I surged with protectiveness. I wanted to deck every self-absorbed, air-headed girlie-jerk who mocked a boy's brave try, the girls who did not see the person beyond their mean refusals. I kept my eyes on my brother, facing him from a chair against the opposite wall, and spent the remainder of the night as my brother's keeper (though he did not know it and never would have liked it), disinterested in my own dance possibilities. Maybe a boy becomes a man who grows a foolish facade in order to guard against giggling girls who deflate his innocent efforts. I would not want to have to ask someone to dance, and have them hold me in contempt because I had risked *their* rejection.

And my brother was protective of me. When I was young I was a careless street crosser, rarely stopping to look both ways. I said I couldn't be bothered and my mother and brother shook their heads at the absurdity of my dangerous aloofness; they tried to instill in me a serious concern for speeding cars and traffic lights. Whenever Clay and I were walking together, and until recently, he would unconsciously extend his arm in front of me, step out to check traffic, and then nudge me along with him across the street safely. He cautioned friends to watch me when he could not be there.

When people outside of our family attempted to impose a blue-pink sensibility on us, my brother and I would smile politely but feel slightly perplexed by the well-meaning adult. Moreover, because we were so close, I felt an unnecessary wedge fall between us when people called attention to our genders, as if it made a difference.

Once, I remember hearing how terrified my brother was when my father's bowling partner Luigi threw my five-year-old brother so high in the air he almost got tangled in the whir of a ceiling fan. I envisioned this large thick-skinned laughing man blind to my small sibling's fright to prove a man's affection among men. My father had never engaged in this tendency—child tossing, while a mother, hands to her face, nervously endures a man's callous child play. My father had played softball with us, built sand castles, and gave us piggybacks; but he had never hurled us in any direction for any reason, much less for fun.

2

My brother was born into a family of women who preferred men; which I believe there was a good reason for at one time (my mother often mentioned that I was of course the exception). Both my mother and grandmother were strong-willed, independent people. My grandmother reigned over every occasion she came in contact with (she ran everything from the grange to the church choir); and she always worked. My mother loved to read, to toss ideas, and was fired up by politics, art, and history. She sought the company of those whose minds would be intellectually exciting, those who would not talk small.

In the fifties there wasn't much compatible female society in the suburbs for a highbrow teenaged mother. And in my grandmother's small rural town powerful women were suspect, and not easily embraced by other women. On the contrary, women were often less kind to the aberrants among their gender, and found opinionated, strong-willed women (mothers no less) a threat to their implicit code of glorified subservience. They were betrayers to their fairer, quieter gender. At a loss for friends among their own, they turned to men for company and recognition, but surely not for definition.

Though the liberated females before me found comfort among men, they had secretly dreamed of more in the men they married; they had loved men who were passive. Back then, before liberation, there seemed to be a dearth of husband varieties; brutes or wimps—men who would hand over their hearts and power to the women they married; or men who would not tolerate an uppity wife's freedom. They chose the romantics and their freedom, but longed, nevertheless, for a masculine kind of courage.

As a result, my brother, this son, this grandson, was prized while being groomed to be a man of vigorous character and romance. He entered into this family with expectation at his heels, with a large order to be rare and strong. In the absence of men who were wont to vigorously claim him among their own, my grandmother and mother claimed him as theirs, and looked up to and banked on the boy. He delivered, but not without a high personal cost. The discovery of his own essence, which may not have always been one of action and tireless responsibility, was buried by their collective expectancy; though I am convinced both my mother and grandmother would have stepped aside, if and when the family men had shown an interest in teaching the boy.

I joined the chorus. I thought my brother was divine. For years, when he was in grade school, he had a paper route, and was the first person I saw get up early and go to work. He'd rise at 5 A.M. on dark winter mornings and walk a mile into town to collect and fold his newspapers, and then return to our neighborhood, where he delivered them, battling bitter cold and scary dogs without complaining. Later he washed dishes at a restaurant after school, and would come home late at night to wash the dishes in our kitchen. He worked harder and more diligently than I had ever seen anyone work; and he always had money he was willing to share.

When I was a teenager, throughout and after our parents' divorce, he gave advice both encouraging and dependable; and after having dropped out of high school, pregnant and despairing, he was the one reason, years later, I eventually went to college. He told me about grants, and how to fill out an application, said I was smart and would be accepted, when I was convinced I had blown my chances.

When my close friend Merrill and I graduated from college, in 1975, my brother and I invited friends to a celebration at my grandmother's house. As we played croquet on the front lawn, a man in a battered sports car veered into the driveway. It was the father of the baby I had given away, who had turned menacing in the years after her adoption. He had stalked me and had called my grandmother to ascertain the whereabouts of his relinquished daughter (my grandmother never told). I stood frozen behind friends, terrified, while my brother walked over to the driver's side of the car, with his mallet in hand, and told my ex-boyfriend in no uncertain terms to leave. When he arrogantly began to get out of the car, Clay stood firm and gave him a final warning. Seconds later, our unwanted guest started up the engine and drove off. Two of my friends who were there on that day have since told me that they have never forgotten that scene. Merrill has said: "When I saw Clay intervene, I was thinking I wanted more than anything a big brother who would protect me like that. He was so sure, so quick to stand up for you."

When I was afraid, I found a comfort in my brother's company like no other. He was not one to nurse or indulge—the suggestion would make him wince; it was his restful, just response that contradicted fear and turned back dread. One afternoon when I was fourteen, I anxiously fought flashbacks which I thought were caused by the pot I had nervously smoked the day before. I went to my brother. "Go with it," he said, smiling, unruffled. "Hey, it's free." I went with it, and it went away. Back then, only he could dismantle my worry. With genial dispassion, he presumed a higher, calmer plane, and confidently dispensed perspective—which has always been for me the best antidote to panic.

And when I met my birthdaughter eleven years after I had given her away, he drove me to our reunion. His moderate presence in the seat next to me during the long ride to her, and his few unambiguous words, invoked reassurance. For him, crises seemed to be an agreeable habitat; he rose to and inhabited with grace the milieu of exigence.

He was as fatherly as anyone had ever been with me—the male against whom I measured all others, because he had the nerve and the grit to remain family when other members fell away. He spoke his mind, was a man of uncompromised action. He was our father, inverted—not passive, not wordless, no coward. But as I got older I was always losing bets waged on his righteousness (he was merely mortal, after all). If my brother said it was true, I argued his word with religious fervor because I was convinced it must be so; and sometimes it wasn't. In the absence of reliable parents, I had made of my brother an irreproachable replacement and, in my mind, had overstated his virtue to the degree I needed it. He embodied a reaction, his and the females who loved him, to the men who failed to come forward and declare their authority, while knowing he would have to betray their ways and his place among them to get there. In our dedicated agenda, we may have forsaken *his* self—ironically abandoning the boy we had protected and the man we so desperately wished him to be.

I always knew my father and I had more in common than he and my brother—we traded Hollywood lore, went to the movies, loved cats, gossiped; and we were both journalism majors in college (though I didn't find this out until a few years before he died). As much as I admired my mother, and as similar as people said we were (our voices, faces, laughs), I also sensed early on that we were fundamentally different, that our emotional ballasts were not the same.

My mother had delicate wrists, triple-A size feet, and slender ankles, which looked barely up to the job of body support. She scoured expensive shoe shops and spent lots of money (when there was little) on imported footwear in order to find a fit. As a kid I wore off-the-rack Keds. I had wide feet and thick ankles (she'd say, "like peasants"), which I decided, when I was about ten, made me sturdy and firm-footed. While I respected my mother more than anyone, in matters of balance I believed I was the more capable version. I began to think that my good physiological foundation was the ground-floor symptom of a larger ability to prevail in tumultuous times. I often felt that, no matter how disorderly life got, I could trust my broad feet to carry me through.

My brother was decidedly my mother's child—they were

more cerebral, bookish, vulnerable, and probably thought my father and I were shallow in our tastes. Back then, even in our unconventional family, a mother-son affinity seemed to breed tension, as if to imply a father's inadequacies, or an overbearing mother's intrusive sway, when neither may have been true. My father seemed to back out of his father figure, never sure how or what he could bring to his son. Maybe he felt, as men often did and still do, that it was his job to pass on some deep wise magic about becoming a man, and he felt foolish because he didn't have any. When my brother grew out of childhood, my father seemed both bitter and confused by my brother's growing tie to his mother; and he seemed scared by his son's impending manhood, as if he would be called on for work he couldn't do. He didn't know how to reach his son; worse, he didn't try.

On the other hand, my father may have understood, despite prevailing lore to the contrary, that a congruence presumed by gender was a hollow theory. But that could not be uttered, much less comfortably observed, in an era when family roles were inflexible. My brother seemed to know it. He has said a dozen times since that when he turned eleven he and my father had nothing much left to talk about; that he accepted it then as he does now.

3

My brother and I walked out of our family into our adulthood differently.

In my early thirties, when my sons were young, I had aches and a kind of loneliness I couldn't get at, wanted to understand, finally had to understand in order to move ahead. (A therapist called it cognitive overdrive, meaning that if I could make sense of something I could get past it.) So I went digging, and found out, all things considered by others besides me, that I had had a blighted childhood; ergo the aches.

I did not know, for instance, that having one's mother and father forget their child's birthday from roughly the age of twelve on may not have been just a matter of personal style; that maybe this might hurt.

Unlike other members of my family, it was and is now again my nature to seek the outside source for counsel. Even when I was a kid (and looked in the *Yellow Pages* for help—Family Services— when our parents had checked out) I did not think it was a failing, but rather capableness—the talent to find what one needed. Getting myself to therapy, in my middle thirties, entailed a vigorous internal debate between me and my family's code of conduct—I had first to banish the assertion I was a spineless plebe for doing so; and then I had to yank myself out of a cozy but corroding ethos and invent another—my own. I gave myself a year to work hard, and emerged from my sessions feeling as if I had been pummeled with bricks—I was frayed and sore. I would sit in my car, both dazed and transformed, for at least fifteen minutes before I could turn the key. But I was lucky. My therapist was astonishingly wise, funny, and kind and she walked me through the fire to the other side.

My family assumed then, and still does, the Proper Bostonian attitude, that therapy or the search for self is indulgent. As if carrying around decades of unattended anger and pain that everyone must dodge and then try to decode isn't?

Fact is, the hunt for one's truth is ultimately a most pervasive act of generosity and leads to very good manners indeed. Because, when one has confronted the fears in the corners, he is released in a way that brings grace and gritty empathy—contorted interiors make for nervous and unpredictable company. Even with the most skilled repressors the unattended psyche leaks menacingly; and without apparent reason meanspirited charges are made. When wounded, the tightly contained bleed a most enigmatic blood, leaving the unwitting offender in a dizzy mess, asking, "From whence has this anger come, whose rage is this anyway, and why is it being directed at me?" I think it is called displacement, a predominantly male affliction in my experience; when emotions are choked back, pushed down, but they ooze or bust out anyway. And because the aggrieved fails to do so, everyone else is forced to do his reflecting for him, moved, as we are, by the sting of the hurt he carelessly inflicts. It's simple, really: If you don't face down your misery it will come looking for you, and spill into the lives of those who are close, the ones you want to hurt the least.

As adults my brother and I have had a terrible time finding our footing as siblings. Without the crises that framed the last half of our childhood together, we are off balance in each other's company. We are reckless, unformatted relatives.

When we were young, we couldn't afford to fight; we relied so desperately on each other to get through the day. Sometimes when we're together we behave like quarrelsome, hurt eight-year-olds, unfinished children fighting and waiting for the adult intervention that vanished too soon.

I loved my father and for a time I admired him. But his lack of follow-through unalterably diminished my faith in him and has, to a notable degree, infected my perception of his gender. If I had not loved a brother so closely and completely, and if he had not protectively loved me back, I might have looked at the country of men and seen only a desolate landscape, and taken with me into adulthood a cynic's detachment. Instead, my view of males, especially boys, has been and is moderated by a sister's intimate, devout compassion and respect, for which my brother was exclusively and absolutely the inspiration.

Part 3

Boyfriends

A coward is incapable of exhibiting love;
it is the prerogative of the brave.

—MAHATMA GANDHI

1

I have traveled among men as a self-assured, outspoken (I've been called irreverent and bitchy) female, which has given me a view of men in the company of such a woman. I know nothing about compromising myself for the sake of a man's attentions or his temporary peace; but I like to think I am warm-hearted above all else.

When I was young, having a brother close in age put me comfortably and regularly in the company of other boys. Males were never a puzzling Them, not the *opposite* but simply another sex, always a part of my social scenery from the start. My brother, his best friend Greg, and I had sleepovers, tumbled down embankments on cardboard, spent summer weeks at our grandmother's house in the country, made lunches, watched Friday night TV together in our pajamas. He and I and his friends and mine bowled, played night games—kick the can, hide-and-seek, buckety-buck—and sometimes our friends got drunk and threw up (as I squeamishly turned away), and we went to the movies en masse.

And we fled from the law. One night Joey and I were partners on the run, when the police had invaded our beer-drinking, trespassing group at Split Rock in the woods on a Saturday night. As soon as we heard crunching footsteps and saw the flashlights, we bolted in all directions. Joey grabbed my hand and we dashed across the street to the back of the sprawling brick convent, where nuns, roused from their prayerful calm by the rustling outside, pulled their curtains to the side and peeked out. He raced up and over the high chain link fence, I followed, tearing my shorts on the way. On the other side, we ran into an abandoned boys' reformatory, stepping over damp, rotting mattresses and broken glass. We waited for our heartbeats to slow down before we emerged into what we thought would be a cop-free zone. Joey and I walked out of the dark into the lit-up street, only to face two unamused officers walking toward us. Joey quickly whispered: "You're Susan and I'm Rich—if they ask."

The officers aimed their lights at us and asked our names. Susan O'Connor, I said, Joey gave his fake name. The officers ordered us to return to our homes at once. Then as we slowly ambled past the cheerless men in blue, Joey upped the ante and said, "Okay, *Linda*, let's go." The cops abruptly turned and yelled, "Hey!" and began to give chase. We slowly picked up speed, then ran fast and hard and never looked back. We landed in my living room, well out of sight of our pursuers, locked the door, hyperventilated, and laughed.

As I got older, my brother's friends continued to see me as a comrade, when I was ready, finally, to be viewed as dating material. Paul Waverly would come over and catch me in the kitchen and divulge to me in vulnerable murmurs that he wanted to go out with Diane Ames, who he thought had gone all the way with Brad, and what should he do, or could I talk to her and find out if she wanted to go out with him? He talked brotherly and I comforted sisterly, all the while seeing heaven in his dark blue eyes and sweet insecurity.

I yearned to be treated as the girl you *wouldn't* bring home to Mom. I wanted to be a boy's breathtaking distraction. I confess I did not know how to flirt or work my gender. I was obtusely autonomous. My mother never told me to downsize my brains and boldness in order to make a boy feel smarter and stronger. So they treated me with dull respect, told me their secrets, came to me for advice, and I sliced oranges for them, listened well, and was their perpetual buddy; but they did not feel infatuated or radiantly awkward in my girlish company.

I read once that the more intelligent and competent a woman is as an adult, the less likely she is to have received an adequate amount of romantic attention as a teenager. Maybe that's because all the energy required for strenuous young love is conserved for later growth and development. And maybe it's just because intelligence and competence are not way cool to most thirteen-year-old boys.

Now, I think my failure to gain the romantic notice of my peers may have been early signs of a male's inability to manage multiple concepts: if she is my friend, then she cannot be my crush. The deficiency in prismatic perception, the ability to see a female as possessing more than one attractive trait, which in turn may appeal to one or more of a boy's tastes, was and continues to be the most notable hazard, vis-à-vis males, of being a female with confidence and smarts. Then again, I wore really dippy glasses back then. . . .

Yet a male who can and is willing to behold all of a female in a first full deep glance has my respect. I am drawn to the guy who can respond to a woman without prorating potential costs to his masculinity or having to carefully deliberate how her self may interfere with his self. When I was twelve, during my days as a *confrère extraordinaire,* a self-assured boy, a heart-stopping exception who seemed eager to explore more of me than my reasonable nature, appeared in our ordinary suburb. His name was Trevor Burns.

He was a California dream. He was visiting his East Coast cousin in the big gray house up on the hill and now he was here—with reckless swatches of West Coast blond hair, stormy-eyed seductive trouble, tight jeans, low voice. This was definitely a BOY. And we girls went ape over him, whispering incessantly about his good looks and his out-of-town maturity.

On that Saturday afternoon in November, gray and boring, being twelve seemed cruel. So when my brother and two of his friends, three stalks of man-boy (late fall gusts still breathing from their wool jackets) erupted into the dull living room, where a fire had smoldered hours before, Trevor Burns was a dream come true. We traded stares, only his stare was suspiciously seasoned, and mine was raw and frightened, but unflinching. I was pulled to the large-limbed, perilous boy.

My brother and his friends shuffled and stopped, unbuttoned and flung coats across the living-room chairs that gaped at the smoking hearth, and leaped with big-booted thuds up the stairs to the attic, where the pool table was and where teens stole kisses and told secrets. Except for Trevor. He stayed behind, he and I attached at the eyes.

Who is this hunk, I thought, with brown bulky arms escaping from sunny-weather T-shirt sleeves? He seemed to know what he was doing but I was lost; only I knew he was the cure. I turned away stunned by my tenderness, picked up a book, and began to fake-read, waiting for his high-voltage gaze to release me.

"So you're Clay's sister?"

"Yeah," I said, eyes affixed to the page.

"I've heard about you," he said, with trained charm, well ahead of his years. "You coming up to play pool?"

I wanted to be near this boy, close enough to smell him, but I couldn't. What would I do? How would I be? What happens when a girl feels this way about a boy?

In the next few days I walked in a gilded path through my house, in between my mother, father, brother, and furniture, carried by sentimental surfer tunes. They didn't know, how could they? This was a feeling for a girl of twelve only. I called up the feeling often during the day, and was transported to another dimension that was immediate, timeless and warm. So he called and we talked and teased.

He was sleeping over my brother's house, he said, which meant my house. Friday. Trevor Beach Boy Burns was sleeping over, in the night, here.

So Friday night came, and we circled each other. When it was time for bed, Trevor stepped up to the attic door, where he would sleep, but first stopped in front of my room. I heard him and grabbed my fleecy bathrobe and answered his faint knock.

"Good night," he said, drawing me close to him.

Then something happened.

I had heard my brother and his friends talk about the altered states of the private parts of boys, if somewhat callously, often admiringly, and always obliquely. Like the way my father had referred reverentially to the sighting of Sputnik. He took us into the starry night and pointed skyward; I peered, intrigued, hoping to see the awesome event, but saw only an empty looming sky. Now it was as if this supernatural rocket had zoomed in under the peach tree in my very own backyard . . .

Suddenly there was movement—a shift in condition—of something beyond my furry turquoise bathrobe, beyond Trevor's britches, between his body and his undershorts. IT was pressing vigorously, hungrily, against me. At first I thought, how difficult it must be for a boy not to be in control of all his body parts, how humiliating, how odd. I could not imagine having an extremity behave on its own accord, independent of me.

And then I was swept away, captivated by the private magical act I seemed to have inspired; and feverishly flattered that he desperately wanted to give it all to only me *now*.

He placed his hands around my fluffy waist and declared his urge. I put my hands on his Pacific coast arms as he lined his body up with mine, hearing my loud heart (hoping he didn't) lulled by the summery California tunes of Trevorness, and feeling for the first time ever the changes that happen to a man-boy when he desires.

"I can't, Trevor, I'm too young," I said, trembling, in a panicky barrage of reason and sense. He persisted. I did too, thus ending at twelve my brief inauguration into lust. If I had not had such a terrifyingly monstrous, fiery urge to give in, I might have.

I have always felt a pull to the primitive bodily differences in men. The puzzle of their physiology, and hormones, the way their backs flare into muscly inverted pyramids, a man's walk, the angles of his face lit by the moon, an escape into the otherworldly waltz of compelling viscera.

It is complicated and draining to keep a man close, in love, because the reasons we attempt it too frequently seem out of reach. The French have a saying, *la petite bonne heure* (small luck); it is the reason, they say, that we get up in the morning. We don't rise out of bed to feed the cat, make coffee, check the mail, or go to work, though certainly there is regular joy in all of the above. We face the day hoping for some indefinable enchantment to visit us. And that is why men and women persevere—we court the transcendent in each other.

I have found powerful tenderness in the hard-earned triumphant groove reached, across the chasm, by a man and a woman.
The chasm is real and it is a hike to the other side. But I have
never considered giving up. Because I know, with a man, the
extraordinary and memorable, wholly inexpressible something is
possible; that there is promise of a day that may deliver the spell,
which will surpass time, place, winter, bills, and bad relatives.
And it is *exclusively* from men that I have received it. It is the
plaintive soprano of Marvin Gaye singing "I Want You" with
stirring, aching credibility, a slow warm dance to a solo saxo-
phone, Trevor Burns's beautiful brave hormones when I was
twelve. It's tough, being and staying with a man, but Jesus God
in heaven, it's the pursuit of that time-stopping impulse to bridge
the ravine that makes me want to try.

For the first time, when I was twelve, I felt how stunningly
out of control, how piercingly vulnerable, wickedly intimate, how
gorgeously sci-fi a male body could be. I still feel that way. It is
an enigma I can count on—the last sure mystery.

2

I reacted to the dissolution of our family with all the aplomb and
forethought of a seriously miserable teenage girl. I ditched what
was left of my withering confidence and created more crises, in
keeping with the wreckage of my mother's mental illness and
father's retreat. I slipped into a subterranean nether world to hide
out where I found men who were more than willing to affirm my
despair.

Teenagers court danger, some more than others. Boys get

arrested. Girls get pregnant. I got pregnant and gave away my baby, and suffered a postpartum, self-destructive indifference.

Looking back, I am often angrier at myself than I am at the men who harmed me. Sometimes I fooled myself back then by believing these boyfriends could be fixed if forgiven and loved enough. But we can't keep them peaceful; that is the work of the sour men themselves and the trained and paid. If it hadn't been me triggering their fury and taking the punches, they would've targeted someone else and been provoked by *their* grotesquely irrelevant offenses, because these men want to do damage. They simply hunt for those willing to serve. And I served. Signed up to be a creep's decoy. Stupidly.

We women have to own up to our part in these terror pacts. I know that once we have been in thick with a lover's rage it is hard to leave, and often impossible to escape. Once I hid under a table in a Laundromat for three hours when I saw my dangerous former boyfriend hunting in the town I was sure he didn't know I lived in; I had become his bad habit, and his withdrawal was slow and jagged. But why did I stay past the second assault; why did I get in so deep?

I have rarely thought of avenging my assailants. Hurting someone now is not going to make me feel good. But defending and rescuing myself long before I did would have.

When I was twenty, after three insulting years, I carefully slipped out the door in the dark while the beast in my bed slept. I never said anything about leaving. I snuck out, because it was the only way. I had made covert plans to go to college in another state, with the urging and support of my brother, and within the first few months felt safe and, once again, the glow of future.

Since then I have been loved well by men and often enough, probably because I eventually regained a tangible view of the person I am. (I credit genes as much as I do my parents for having cultivated my confidence when I was very young. They said I was perceptive and secure, before I was old enough to understand what the words meant. I remember looking them up in our dictionary.) This self-knowledge—and an unforgiving memory of past ordeals—have generated an advanced radar system for sensing what I am thoroughly sure I do not want or need in a man; and what I will not, no matter what, tolerate.

I have allowed myself ruthless reductionisms in this area. I can tell if a man is hiding his terror of women not far under his skin. Big alarms go off if I sense a man wants me to be quiet, calmer, or less opinionated; or if he wants me to be his mother. A giant door slams if he is inordinately hygienic, or calls women "gals" (the painstaking attempt of a man who can't quite get there). I can't imagine being attracted to a man who persuades what little hair he has to conceal hairlessness elsewhere (What's so bad about bald? Bald is good.); or a man who habitually drinks more than his body's water weight in alcohol (My tolerance for drinkers is now in the negative numbers.). And I would have little to say to a man who growls at hockey games, feels as one with the GOP, or prefers bony women, i.e., hipless boy bodies. I want to say: "This is what we have to offer you guys— adipose curves, bellies designed to carry babies—the slim hips and flat stomachs you can provide for yourselves."

I sprint swiftly in the other direction if a man is miserly, with his spirit or his money. As he got older, my father clutched so tightly to what was his, and gave so rarely, that he made those of us who dared to want feel criminal; the expression of need was considered a character flaw. He loathed waste and was careful not to buy more of anything than was exactly needed; hence no excesses. When my mother got sick, she ironically echoed his contempt for nurturance—it was for the feeble among us. Growing up with a begrudging father led me on a beeline to men with a near fanatical habit of squandering everything often. In the company of free givers my needs were camouflaged; I could want without feeling weak.

And most importantly, if I sense a man's smoldering, oblique anger, I disappear carefully but quickly.

Too, I am convinced, through my experience, that men worth kissing or keeping company with really do prefer noncompliant women. I understood this for the first time when I saw my fourteen-year-old son react to a female friend who cozied up to him, flapped her lashes, and breathlessly asked for a piece of his gum.

He was seriously miffed and said, "Yeah, if you ask in a normal voice."

At first I did not understand why he was so steamed. But then I figured when a guy gets really masculine with me—or when people become their race, religion, disability, or shirt size—I get steamed too. When someone operates with only one of their many distinctions, my impulse is to say, "Can you try that again, this time with all cylinders?" It is an affront to be offered so little of a self.

José's friend was presenting an abridged version of her personhood, moderated by gender, and that meant she might expect him to respond in kind with his own male-defined variety. And my young son didn't know how. He didn't know what the corresponding part of that behavior was, but he knew he couldn't or didn't want to work it up. For the guy who wants the privilege and protection of his gender, coyness in gals is testosterone-affirming. But males who want to be seen as people first feel instantly freed from contrived intergender social sports, such as chivalry (which presumes a female to be a damsel, instead of a peer).

Though I do believe, knighthood notwithstanding, that a

return to civility is seriously needed. When I have taken public transportation in recent years I have observed, on far too many occasions, pregnant women standing. In the aloofness of the unobliging seated commuters I smell backlash. On your feet, soldier, the suggestion seems to be. Hey, you wanted equality (reproductive rights, women in combat), equal *this*. Obviously, anyone who appears uncomfortable ought to be offered a seat by someone less so. Such protocol has nothing to do with gender and everything to do with simple consideration.

I have found that evolved men, who know the difference between kindness and gallantry, feel gratefully emancipated in the company of females who have a life. But the best-kept secret of all is that men, the worthy among them, can't get enough of an uncompromised woman. She is consistently beguiling, the ultimate anti-Mom, not self-sacrificing and all-forgiving, but self-interested and conditional. If a pliant woman's deference is perpetually on tap, her love is not noticed, much less valued, when given. A woman who habitually bends robs a romance of its appetite and removes one person from the affair; a pall of presumption and incessant devotion would neutralize anyone's ardor—except of course a man who is hungry for Mother. For the guy who wants to be a lover (and friend) to the woman he loves—and not a father, son, or Svengali—a self-possessed woman—not to be confused with the guise of the hard-to-get—is a prize.

Too, androgynous men can be identified not only by their ease with secure women but in the presence of homosexual men as well. Liberated gay men, who have turned sexuality on its head, provide a cool, spacious, carpeted locker room where heterosexual men can get out of their clunky, noisy gladiator gear and slip into something comfortable—ungraded manhood. Nobody is trying to outman anyone else here, the sanctions are lifted, it's a noncompetitive come-as-you-are kind of thing. Men who are edgy in a gathering of more than one female, tense in the presence of gays, are often handicapped in their ability to perceive the person behind the gender, his and theirs. A homophobe is embarrassingly confessional. He reveals far more of *his* inadequacies than he had ever intended.

After years of renouncing anti-women men, I have realized that it is, in fact, not women some men find dreadful, but a flattering amount of vulnerability men have to them—to a misogynist a woman matters very much, too much. A male's misogyny is a measure of the damage he has suffered and the danger he still feels if he relinquishes control to a woman, who he believes had held and continues to hold the terrifying power to dislodge his grip. He will not go there again, he promises himself, without a well-engineered, often abrasive defense against the powerfully offending gender; he will not venture forward without an all-inclusive policy statement against the wrongdoers. In my experience, a few earnest minutes of a neophyte's analysis can reveal the wound. The man who leans toward misogyny is a person who has had an experience from which he has emerged with what he believes is an informed, educated grudge, if he owns up to his bias to begin with. To say that a man hates women is far too facile. A misogynist is battle-scarred.

A sexist, on the other hand, relies on crude multimedia images to feed his negligible cache of info about and interest in females. He has no wish to delve deeper, to put down the *Playboy* and contemplate or question cursory gender roles; enlightenment, for him, is about higher wattage. He cannot stop ogling women long enough to actually see them. He has not had an adverse encounter with a woman by virtue of the fact that he would not recognize one if he had had it; if his affair fails he'll just keep trolling until he meets a woman willing to cry uncle to his aggressive simple-mindedness. It's his disinterest in women that infuriates. Bottom line: he's way more concerned with other men's perceptions of him than he is with what he considers a woman's cute opinion. A sexist is dense and detached. A misogynist, if somewhat gutless, is at least engaged; he is injured and angry.

One Saturday when I was twelve I went to the Beacon Hill Theater to see the movie *Tom Jones,* starring Albert Finney; by the third straight showing my friends had long gone and I still couldn't tear myself away. I sat in the balcony, alone, magnetized to the man on the screen. Our Tom was at the mercy of his considerable affections—he was impassioned, venturesome, engaging, as generous with wenches as he was with ladies. He was no taut, moralizing man; he wore no fortifying disguises—he was, above all, reachable, warmly, mortally reachable. At the movies that day, entranced as I was by Finney's Tom, I discovered the alchemy of eros—an attraction not born of gain, experience, consequence, or motive, but simply the way my heart was won.

Someone once told me, and I believe it's true, that if you feel totally in control you're not in love. To discover deep romance, one must be willing to risk defenseless and frightful exposure, no matter how many faith-shattering setbacks; moreover you've got to care enough to want to try. And it is *that* heroic wager of the heart that has endeared me to the men I've loved.

3

My mother is someone who should not have slept alone, yet my father insisted from the start on having his own bedroom. Every night he went to his darkened room without her. She left her metal-framed bed on the other side of the wall to join him by invitation late at night and sometimes on Sunday mornings. Early in their marriage I remember seeing my mother leaning against my father's back in the kitchen before supper, her hands gently sprawled over his shoulders, and then my father, preoccupied, would walk away without giving back. Watching my mother awkwardly negotiate for her husband's warm attention left me with a gut-level desire for men who yield to their romance. I steer clear of the nonresponsive.

One day at college after a four o'clock lit class, I stopped in to see a friend who was working at a restaurant. She said, "Robert Windsor told me he wants to meet you." With that, three other waitresses gathered in a huddle, clicked their tongues, and swooned. "I wish Robert Windsor wanted to meet *me*," said one. "Luckeee," said another.

A few weeks later, after some discreet maneuvering by mutual acquaintances, Robert and I found ourselves sitting next to each other among friends at the Red Roof Tavern on a Friday night. I had just sat down when the table seemed to be encircled in a drama I didn't get, prompted, I found out later, by the surprise visit of the irate ex-girlfriend of one of the men who sat with us. Robert coolly began to sort out the predicament, by both comforting the hostile girlfriend and defending his friend, the man who happened to be with another woman. He was a sovereign presence, calmly defusing what could've been a messy scene, with an unassuming charity for all. His sense of fairness was instantly appealing.

Over the next few weeks I realized he was a man I could love; he was generous, attentive, unafraid of his romance, a handsome Cyrano who was willing to risk full-hearted affection, with the same kindness he had shown during our first encounter at the Tavern.

After we had lived together for several months, amid my fearful discouragement Robert removed an enormous, exquisitely carved mahogany Victorian bed from an abandoned house in the woods past midnight. This would be our bed, he said.

Throughout my college years, he tracked and supported my academic achievements with pride. He taped my radio shows, went with me when I interviewed people for articles, and stood by me when one controversial piece got me booted out of a bar. He made a deal with a friend and presented me with my first car, and fixed it when it broke down. We shared an apartment, and one summer crossed the country in his convertible. He was my main source of encouragement and renewal after I had lost a family, a baby, and had been bruised by men; and his affectionate respect restored my comfort with closeness. He believed I could write, said I was beautiful. Kept my secrets.

During my senior year in college I had ambitiously campaigned for a position with a TV station in New York City—I sent what I had hoped would be attention-getting monthly letters. After I graduated in May, without having heard from the station, I spent the summer living alone in a rooming house and working at a restaurant on the beach while I contemplated a career move. A local radio station had offered a job in the meantime, but in late summer the TV station finally came through. After a summer apart, Robert and I had become close again, and I was torn. The decision seemed bigger than a change of address:

it was a matter of Future, the next Big Step. With the encouragement of friends, I eventually decided I could not say no to the city—and accepted the job I had lobbied so hard to get.

On the day I moved to New York, Robert drove me to the train station, and though we had talked of our continuing a long-distance relationship, we both knew without saying it that our time was over. We hugged and, with resignation, he watched me step onto the train and into a life far from his; and by the time I settled into a window seat to wave goodbye, he was gone. I am convinced, though he had urged me to stay, that he knew leaving is what I should've done. For a while, we kept in touch but eventually grew apart.

Looking back, I cannot imagine a better man to have loved and been loved by during those years in my life. What we had had brought me back to myself—out of the abyss.

As much as my father has informed my choice in men, the men I've loved since have contributed more. They have revealed possibilities I could not have known had I not known them. Much of how I felt with Robert, unlonely, lovingly recognized, is how I wanted to feel. I would look for it again.

Part 4

Sons

1

I have been attracted to artists, romantic men, perhaps in part because of their comfort with a conceit I coveted. They served themselves and their art without ambivalence and were not afraid of their passion or of the solitude that the making of art seems to require. Now as I look forward to a calm exile of my own (unobligated middle age) I realize I have kept the art nearby, in order not to forget.

When writer and mother Anne Morrow Lindbergh deserted her family, briefly, for the solitude of the sea, she discovered that "the running of a house with its thousand details; human relationships with their myriad pulls . . . run counter to creative life, or contemplative life. . . ." I wait, like a jumpy kid, for a time when my life is free of what Lindbergh calls the "centrifugal activities"—the practical and common interferences of daily life; and have, in the meantime, retained at least glimpses, in the intimate company I keep, of the kind of artful contemplation I have yet to fully fathom.

Too, I find the androgyny and sense of self I see in creative men appealing—the constraints of gender seem to be overshadowed by what I've observed to be the artist's inner-driven desire to express a whole, albeit complex self. And certainly there has been an element of the impulsively amorous Tom Jones in the men I've loved.

The upside of being loved by a sensual man is that he swears he finds all of what he wants, including the moon and the stars, in his irresistible lover; the downside is that his lover feels chronically alluring and the weight of a galaxy when tending his heart. Sometimes I fantasize about the emotionally compact, undistractible guy, who is married to his business—a guy who's titillated by long, consecutive phone calls to important people, who doesn't need, or want, a woman in whom to gloriously lose himself. "I'd love to, but I've got to balance the checkbook," are words I've never heard. Instead I've been with men who readily abandon the immediate and useful for higher carnal ground if, in their lover's glance, they *think* they see a mere invitation to do so.

I'd like to believe I could have it both ways. An impassioned man who has his limits, days when he just isn't in the mood for heavenly merging. And then I would have my days when I did not feel like the sole sponsor of his pivotal pleasure. As far as I can figure there are many reasons, 107 and counting, for men to want sex (it's Tuesday, he's 1. sad, 2. happy, 3. confused, or his taxes are done); whereas for me I can think of only one—that I feel like making love. (Though some guys tell me I have this all wrong. It's women, they say, who bring the subtext into the bedroom. But that is another book.)

However, I cannot imagine being with a man whose greatest purpose is me—being desired is one thing, but providing a raison d'être is quite another. The soul of a man who guards his sphere of creation and imagining cannot be replenished by love alone. An artist's muse is elusively—gratefully—elsewhere.

And maybe I see in these artful men what I loved most about my father—his lively, loyal respect for his passion. Despite a consuming postwar suburban expectation to do otherwise, Sam did not throw away or resentfully silence his jazz. I remember feeling privileged as a kid because I had a father who was uniquely self-satisfied, possessed of an appealing talent. He did not brood and hurry in the mornings (he slept late and we were ordered to walk softly until at least eleven on weekends), and he did not return, spent, at the end of the day—by supper his momentum had just begun.

Keeping his music close and alive allowed Sam, I believe, to bring to his family in the early years an unembittered man still in touch with his spirit-driven purpose. We seemed to sense the connection. Maybe he knew it too. Maybe he knew that if he gave up jazz he wouldn't have much to give.

I first saw Thomas when we both worked at a television station in New York City. I was talking with a man in an office off a corridor when I looked up and saw the most exquisite-looking man I had ever seen walk by. The colors of his face were uncommonly beautiful; his intense, sable eyes and smooth coffee-colored skin were framed by shining, loose, charcoal curls; his pale mauve lips were full, perfect. And he walked slowly, confidently, with his hands in the pockets of his loose khakis. I furtively stepped to the door and watched him visit a mutual friend, Kenny, in another office and then leave. I excused myself from the company of the person with whom I was discussing business, dashed into Kenny's office, closed the door swiftly behind me, and demanded to know: WHO was that? "Kenny," I said, "he is *gorgeous!!* I am going to marry that man." I hyperventilated, wide-eyed, pacing. "Who, Tom Garcia?" he asked, laughing, amused by my sudden, slobbering fixation.

A week later, even before I spoke to him, I had a dream of us riding a bus on our way uptown to the Museum of Natural History, with our two small boys.

After what seemed like an eternity of indirect inquiry (among mutual associates), and stolen stares in front of the elevator, the mysterious, vivid Thomas called. On our first date I could not eat. Months later he told me he knew I was the one, that was why he waited so long to call. He told me he had to take care of business, make room for the woman he knew he would love for a long time.

Thomas was as brilliant and creative as he was appealing, though he was never a man to work his looks. He had an artist's hands—solid and smooth, perfectly formed—he turned lines into fluid renderings; the colors he chose sprang from the page. He turned intricate junk from city streets into elaborate collages, wrote poetry, and translated complex ideas into absorbing, visual wisdom. Over the next year he showed me the best of the city; we went to jazz clubs, napped in the sun in Central Park, and visited all of the museums all of the time. Sometimes after we had walked the floors of the Metropolitan wrapped in each other's arms, we collapsed on marble benches, back to back, and then we would leave because it had been too long, a couple of hours, since we had been able to passionately kiss.

I saw a thoughtfulness in him I was sure would be a gift to his children; he protectively whisked kids off city streets out of harm's way, he ran for ambulances and intervened without thinking when someone was in trouble. He possessed a rare blend of bravura and tenderness. He stepped out of himself in an instant when he saw the need, and responded with warm reason.

When I became pregnant, we were ecstatic.

But we did not marry. Despite my emphatic, if metaphorical, insistence on wanting to wed Thomas upon first sight, I don't remember ever really wanting to marry men (though I am a sobbing fool at other people's weddings). I never once had a bridal vision. When I played with my Barbie dolls I preferred the career wear—tight gray skirts and wide-brimmed hats. My grandmother once bought me a bride doll and I cut up her dress into a fancy cocktail number, and made a shawl of the veil. When I was a girl I did not dream of having my father hand me, a-fluff in stiff white massive dress, over to the waiting hand of a man. The entire wedding concept, for me, reeked of discomfort on a large scale. Why would I want to navigate a long aisle in prickly lace, tight shoes, and lacquered hair, while faking a celestial contentedness? Moreover, I was not the least bit interested in having dozens of people listen in on or a designated pro underwrite my personal romantic plans with a man. I had always wanted to make my own rules in affairs of love.

My earliest idea of adult love was of me living in an atelier with a fellow artist in Paris (as a kid I liked the pictures in my Madeline books), materially impoverished, yet rich in passion. Then I wanted to be Elizabeth Taylor in *The Sandpiper*—living idealistically with a son in an artsy shack on the ocean, surrounded by plants and lanterns and paints. I would have a tempestuous, slightly scandalous affair with an irresistible man, throw fabulous beach parties, have little money, great friends, and much good karma.

And when our son was born, two years after we met, that is what Thomas and I had—no money, a warm, generous circle of friends, love, and art.

The hospital swarmed with loud, festive visitors on the afternoon our first child arrived—champagne bottles were smuggled into my room—and gifts of lingerie, flowers, and gourmet edibles were heaped onto my bedside table. Agitated nurses kept urging our calamitous, jovial company to please wait outside, or at least to celebrate in shifts. Thomas, still clad in hospital blues, walked on air from my room, through the hallway, to the nursery and back, receiving, en route, the effusive congratulations of all.

Within an hour of José's birth, my friend Eleanor came into the room, where I was sprawled on my hospital bed drunk with fatigue and euphoria, and with my face hanging off the edge of the pillow, I mumbled tearfully, "I have a son." Eleanor said I sounded as if I had just received the long-awaited gift of a lifetime, and that she had no idea I had wanted a boy. "You spoke as if you already knew the child. You didn't say you had a boy, or a baby, but a son, he was yours and you were his, as if it had always been."

After having lost my first child to adoption, I realized years later that I was hell-bent on claiming this baby as my own as soon as he had become merely an idea—a miraculous one. And besides, whenever I imagined the children I would have I saw boys.

I think I believed, though I never said this, that I would be a better parent to male children. Having boys meant, at least, that the vast supply of psycho-emotional mother-daughter hazards I had known—rejection, competition, and disillusion— might be somewhat diminished. My relationship with my mother had become a mangled fusion caused by her sickness and desertion; and the baby I had lost and whose absence had caused such pain was a daughter. I was apprehensive about bringing the lamentable failure of female merging to yet another generation.

But my brother and I had shared an abiding love and closeness; it was unambivalent, unopposing, mutually protective, and deep. Loving a boy seemed simpler. I knew I could do that.

I know many women who say they are relieved to have sons. A mother-child union is intense enough, they confess, without complicating that intimacy with same-sex enmeshment. There's more air between mothers and sons—a difference in gender provides some breathing room in what otherwise can be an overwhelmingly close bond and can ameliorate a mother's androgynous tendencies.

For most of my life I have felt neither male nor female, and both. Sometimes when I am in the company of other women I find myself nervously wondering whether they know as I do that I can be as male-ish as some of the men we complain about. I often want to talk solutions, take action, I don't like to shop, I'd prefer to disappear when people get sick, I don't cry easily or often, and I've never felt like I wanted to lie about my age or weight (as if the disclosed data might devalue me).

Whenever I spend more than six minutes altering my appearance, I feel like a cosmetic quack. In the mirror I do not see a seamless enhancement of dormant beauty, but a person whose face has been concealed with red smudges and black lines. I keep thinking I should—that I'm missing some fun—but I just don't get the regimen of makeup (though I have always liked playing with colors). And when I wear anything that pinches, cleaves, or clings to my torso I feel as awkward, irate, and foolish as the fraudulent Daphne (a.k.a. Jack Lemmon) in *Some Like It Hot.* I have all but lost my taste for jewelry, and I resent having to abandon my jeans and soft shirts for formal adult female wear (and fail to see the point in this the older I get).

Not that I do not love being a woman. I do. Especially when I was pregnant and had babies; when I am dishing and howling with my girlfriends; when I am alone with the man I love; during the Vietnam War when I didn't have a number; in the schoolyard when I didn't have to fight, or at dances when I didn't have to risk gut-seizing ridicule. But when I am forced to dress up, when I can't hitchhike and want to, or walk home alone at night, I feel like a person trapped in a woman's body. So the sexual identity of my children has never felt like a drastic divergence from the gender I am.

Yet with boys my mission seemed clear, more focused, much needed. Having sons sometimes feels like the difference between a job with the Peace Corps and corporate merging; venturing into underdeveloped land armed with useful advances versus joining with one's own to cultivate leverage. And for those of us with an exhaustingly optimistic urge to counsel and crusade, sons are the cause célèbre. Mothering boys was the perfect forum, justified and suitable, for my lingering yen to give loving protection to and make a difference in the other gender. If I was to be comprehensively engaged in the care of my children (and after my mother's defection, and having forfeited my motherhood once before, I could or would not do it any other way) I wanted, I suppose, to have my motherwork elevated to hard-earned, socially conscious heights.

Thomas was a more natural parent to our newborn babies than I; he held them as if they were a part of his body, bathed and sang to them. He was an unambivalent, affectionate parent. He always kissed his boys full on the lips, hugged and held them, expressed his love unabashedly. When our first son was born he made a block print picture, with gushing poetry announcing the arrival of Skates (so called because of the sliding movements of his tiny feet across and inside my pregnant belly). Before that he was the man every woman should have in a delivery room; he was calm, unsqueamish, amusing, and involved—so much so, the hospital staff was sure he worked in the medical field. My father, on the other hand, continued to play cribbage with my grandfather while my grandmother drove and literally held in the baby my mother could hardly contain on the way to the hospital.

Thomas cooked, often pastallios (a Puerto Rican specialty—his mother's recipe), causing a kind of wild creative combustion, affecting what he called his "Julio Childé" persona, ingredients flying, smells wafting. He designed and sewed toys and Superman capes and karate gi's, he decorated elaborate birthday cakes for his kids.

There is no question that my sons' WASP heritage has been enriched by their Latino ancestry. Latino and WASP cultures are polar—we of reserved expression, spine-tightening winters, and oxford cloth can only benefit from an infusion of the obliging demonstrativeness of the culture which brings us sambas, salsa, temperate weather, and passion. For my sons, the machismo component was negligible, as they were once removed, generationally, from their traditional Puerto Rican grandfather; and during the early years their father was notably free of the affliction. Still José and James always seemed to see it for what it was: an annoying, not wholly credible type.

Years ago I was awakened to my own rigid protocol by a terrifying lapse in good sense that could have caused disaster. My young son was toddling swiftly to the curb and I found myself not screaming at him to stop. Instead I raced toward my child in polite silence because I believed that yelling in public was boorish. (As a result, I immediately enrolled myself in a crash course in gut-level response, by instantly shedding all mannerliness when it came to protecting my kids. My friend Merrill, of Anglo origin too, would say many horrid crimes have been committed in the name of good taste.) Nevertheless, selective deprogramming notwithstanding, good manners can serve as so much social equity when crossing class lines and visiting diverse cultural circles. But the spirited affection, visual sensitivity, and emotional liberty my kids have inherited from their father's culture have served them well.

The free(er), more vital expression of Caribbean character, moored by a steadfast Protestant mannerliness, began to feel like a perfect merging—full-bodied chili, if you will, with a soothing dollop of sour cream.

My older son worked his way into his individuality only after a headstrong detour into Latino identification (a useful digression, I believe), during which time he negated all and any WASP affiliations or tastes. Now he declares he is José, simply, a "product of my heritage, personality, upbringing, environment, genetics, class, culture, experiences, fashion statements, et cetera. . . ." But he observes with humor the differences in his dual heritage. And he shares them often with me.

Both José and James have more often than not ended our telephone conversations by saying, "I love you." (In my family of origin, such casual dispersing of emotion would've been considered common and cramped, cheapened by the frequency of its expression—my father could not release the words until his seventh decade.) For them, it is a punctuation they have grown accustomed to, as much, I believe, from their father's early liberal affection as from an inadvertent comfort they feel with me, because I grant them space—the requisite distance conceded by all good Anglophiles. We have in our house always, even if the door is ajar, knocked and deferentially ducked before being welcomed in.

A couple of years ago José ended our talk with the usual, and I did not respond in kind, right away. He was semiseriously annoyed. The week before I had told him how much I loved him; I amplified and elaborated, clarifying with precise measurements how deep and broad my love for him was. But tonight on the phone, he just wanted the words, not an analytical sonnet.

"Do you love me? You don't love me. You never say you love me. You WASPs are ruled by rationality." And then, affecting his best tight Whiteman voice, " 'You *know* I love you. Why must I state the *ob*vious? It is known, is it *not?*' Couldn't you be more Rican and just say it? I always say it. . . ."

So now, on the phone, I have started to say it (not just as a rejoinder). And they of the male gender have taught me how. I say it to good friends, to my kids, to my lover—before they go on trips, when they are facing a tough day, sometimes for no good reason at all. Not always, not often, but when I feel it and want them to know.

And José and James are unself-consciously affectionate. I, of the Yankee careful-affection genus, was no huggy bunny before I had kids. Having spent one year too many in a physically abusive relationship when I was in my teens didn't help; and during and after the cold disintegration of my family, I had found it far less confusing to simply not touch at all, except for nonambivalent carnal contact. In my first year of college, as we piled into the back seat of a friend's car, I jumped when another woman's knee touched mine. I was more startled by my wacky reaction than I was by the brief touch of another body.

When my oldest son was about five and went to give his grandfather a birthday embrace, José bounced off him like a tennis ball off a wall. My father was stiff and unresponsive. When José asked why my father didn't hug back, I explained, "It's not you, my love, it's just that as a child Sam was never hugged, and so he is not used to it." My son was baffled.

José and James hug everyone all the time, it's a natural part of their greetings and regards. And now I am the harlot of huggers—I embrace semi-strangers, making up for the cold-boned years—feeling a tiny bit deviant nearly every time. As he got older, my father began to hug too, gently, tentatively, like a preadolescent discovering kisses in the dark.

In our final years together, a terrible sorrow overtook Thomas— due, perhaps, to the grueling familiarity and demands of family life and my too frequent lack of tolerance and understanding. I was still in reactive mode—too often shut down and contaminated by the corrupt translations of my own shattered family. In my late twenties I wasn't yet sure who I wanted to be, and clung to and imitated, badly, the ill-fitting, albeit only, ethos I had known—that of a crumbling, impassive, privately suffering clan.

What giving I had I gave to my kids, fiercely and carefully defining my motherhood, indeed defining me, so as not to become the aloof parents I had lost. Too often, I was exclusive and occupied. Retrospectively, in the broad, ceaseless span of adult growth, I was young still.

And Thomas never seemed to adapt fully or easily to our move from his beloved, busy New York to heterogeneous, sedate New England. But as much as he tried to contend with our transplanted growing family, I believe he fought even more the effects of combat—his collapsed spirit was in part a casualty of Vietnam (he enlisted at seventeen to escape a bedeviled father). He seemed to be losing sight of his love for himself, lost, I believe, in the trauma of wars—from the conflicts in his traditional Puerto Rican family which were so harshly alien to his nature and then overseas amid gunshots. This was a boy who *never* should have gone to war; and he was a man who had to invent himself, believing, as he did from the start, that he could make art, despite a lack of training and a family's encouragement, and get paid for it, which he was doing when we met. During our last year together I would look at him and see a sadness that haunted me, that I felt both responsible for and helpless to change.

But beyond our drama, I began to see in our sons a restive sadness—their bewildered young response to the tension engulfing their parents, and consequently them—and I knew I had to make changes. That meant, then in my mind, the final reason to end the relationship. I never thought of staying together "for the kids." I often think that by the time the children are the only reason for a marriage to continue, it is time to part *for their sakes.* Young children cannot grasp adult emotional life, but what little sense they can make of the indecipherable, cloying unhappiness around them, hastily, immaturely translates into their worst imaginable fate. They become engorged with worry and fear, because they don't know how to know. The strain in our house, by the end, was uprooting them.

When we separated, after ten years together, Thomas crawled inside his wounds, and I became the single parent of our two children.

2

There is no one family configuration better than another for raising children. What matters is . . . are the children respected, nurtured, encouraged and loved?

—JUNE STEPHENSON
Men Are Not Cost-Effective

When I found myself in the position of having to support two children, ages four and five, I was unafraid. I'd felt, since the dubious years in a family dominated by a mother's tricky psyche and a father's retreat, that I could handle anything if I could just know what it was I must overcome. Just tell me what it is I have to do, and I will do it, is how I felt (and still do). It's the strained uncertainty of waiting for help that may not come, dangling in a state of suspended need, that feels intolerable. As I faced the upheaval of my second family, I was steadied by purpose; this time, *I* would not be a parent who would fall with it.

I never fought hard or legally for child support. Probably because I had known no firm example of a paying man. I assumed, as I had since my early teens, that whatever money I needed, for whatever reasons, would come from me; and by the time I was in my early thirties I had a dependable record of self-support. Too, I felt more than adequately compensated by their father agreeing to have the children live with me. It seemed greedy, mercenary almost, to consider my children redeemable, a source of income; I had so much, so thoroughly what I wanted— them. From the moment I became their only guardian I felt unabashedly in full possession of my kids. Though I welcomed other people's interest in and care for my children, the obligation was and has always been mine alone. I knew that. We all knew that. They were mine, I was theirs. Money was a detail.

It was not until many years later that I realized my experience of expectation, for better or worse, had, in fact, become part of my sons'.

I first looked into collecting about two years after I was separated. The lawyer was discouraging: he said it would take lots of time and money. I didn't have either. (We struggled financially, but my kids told me later they thought we were rich. José said he thought I kept our considerable stash in what was the fuse box in the wall of our tiny kitchen, where, in fact, we kept merely fuses.)

The second time, years later, I went through the IRS and had everything but the necessary information. This time I told the kids, and they pleaded with me to let it go. "He doesn't have any money, Mom. We can make it without him." Their sympathy for what they viewed as their father's hardship, the negotiable cost of *their* support, was troubling. "You guys," I said, "providing for children is not something you do if you have money left over. It is the first thing you do if you have any money at all."

In protecting their tie with their father, by not making a case, and by bringing low hopes with me from my past, I had, it seemed, accepted a bad example in front of my kids. They forgave him, literally at their own expense.

After years of what I eventually understood was his struggle to make private sense of his father's negligence, my fourteen-year-old son stood in the middle of our kitchen and, in a free-floating epiphany, announced to himself and within earshot of me: "I get it. It has nothing to do with money. It's taking responsibility for your kids."

Monthly payment to the other parent is a relevant, extremely significant kind of debt. It is one way a noncustodial parent can regularly declare his committed love to his children. When a father fails to pay, the message is twofold. He is showing his children that being an adult does not have to include being responsible for one's kids. And secondly, being responsible for you, his own, doesn't change that.

In the end, parents must know that the price of their financial cowardice is far more costly than the sum of support payments. A nonpaying father is not just a cad hoarding his cash, but a parent withholding from his child a lesson he has the power to teach—how to be a trustworthy man. For every parent who fails to send the check, there is probably a child or two who will pay the bigger debt of having to find his way to adulthood without first getting his father's blessed invitation in the mail.

I took a job as an editorial assistant (at $4.75 an hour) at a magazine I had been free-lancing for for the past couple of years while waitressing for regular money. It was the first full-time day job I had held since my children, then five and six, were born; and I left them reluctantly. But I was grateful for work in a field I loved. Since I had become a mother I had taken jobs that would give me time to be with my kids; I had worked mornings at legal assistance while they were at day care and I wrote articles while they napped at home in the afternoon. I took a teaching job with a private educational firm that gave me four weeks on, then two weeks off; I quit a waitressing job when the manager kept giving me the afternoon shift (when hired, I had made it clear I wanted nights). I had sought the kind of employment that would allow me to indulge my primary interest—being a mother to my kids—and I wrangled with logistics to make it happen.

But I felt then as I do now that it is important for my sons' mother to work. Not only to bring something to the table besides the nurturance of the other people at that table, but also to show us that I am capable of being an economic player. There are of course practical alternatives and sundry exceptions, but I have always felt that, if we expect men to be both nurturers and providers, we must be willing to be both as well.

Through a series of vacated positions, within months I had become an associate editor and was making more money than I ever had. I worked hard, showed up on time, rarely missed work but promptly left at four-thirty every day, much to the seething annoyance of the publisher, a bulbous woman (with bulbous eyes and ears, bulbous breasts and cheeks and booming voice). She had a rocky temperament and a mighty drive. She finally called me into her office and expressed her irritation.

"This is a deadline business, your contributions are invaluable here, but you can't walk out at four-thirty, there's work to do, that's all there is to it," she said. "I know you're a single parent, but you've got to be here, everyone else is." I told her I met my deadlines (in fact I was usually early), completed my assignments and then some, worked through lunch every day but Friday, and that I wasn't about to pretend I didn't have a family, or that I wasn't the only parent my kids had. I did not want to be bullied into believing that an unbalanced devotion to work would be the only ticket to career success (to say nothing of general well-being).

Moreover, when it was workable, I integrated my parenting with my job—I practiced shameless nepotism, much to the delight of my kids. I decided to publish a poem and drawing about spring my kids collaborated on, and when I did a story on ice cream, they were the adorable kids pictured with the big dripping cones illustrating the piece. I took them with me when I did stories on the science center, a dairy farm, and the sheep fair.

My boss had been a single parent at one time, too, she said; she wanted me to understand she'd been there. Hire a live-in, that's what *she* did. (And put her where in my four-room apartment—in the closet?) Or take the time on the weekends to be with my kids. That worked for her. She took them skiing, her three daughters, every Saturday and Sunday. (And I should squander food money on ski lift tickets too?) She didn't get it.

I promised her I was a better employee because of my priorities; that she wouldn't want a worker who didn't value her family, would she? "I'm leaving at four-thirty," I said, "until my coworkers complain." (They never did.) "Get out," she boomed with a slight grin, "you make me crazy."

At thirty-three, after having spent nearly ten years sharing daily life with a man, I looked forward to a long stretch of singlehood; to a time when I could be lusciously unconcerned with the intimate life (and myriad feelings) of another adult within my home. For as long as I could remember I had kept habitual company with a guy partner of varying significance—I had been somebody's girlfriend since I was sixteen years old.

But for the first few months, at regular intervals, I was pulverized by sorrow—for the loss of the man I loved, my children's father, and our four-person family. I watched José and James try to make sense of their father's absence, and felt for the first time that when they hurt I could not make it better. I missed living with the only person who loved my kids as much as I—of easily releasing half the weight of responsibility for them to another equally devoted person. Suddenly there was no one to share the small miracles of our sons' incremental growth or unfolding personalities. There was no one to worry with when they got sick. When I was away from them, I could no longer enjoy full relief, the way I had when I knew their father was watching over them. I began to feel like a weathered figurehead, ceaselessly navigating front and center on the prow of a ship which was hauling incredibly valuable cargo. As familiar and manageable as unassisted obligation had been, I had known enough of a parental partnership with Thomas to want more, and to miss the down time afforded by being one of two in charge.

In the kitchen after the kids went to bed, I would lean against the counter and relive and digest in unforgiving detail the aching, incurable break with the man I loved, and knew I always would because he is my children's father. In the dark, still and alone, I finally and permanently released my hope of the full family I had wanted to give my kids, and I would double over in pain. Forcing the reflection and swallowing it whole, again and again, accelerated an urgently needed recovery: I had two children to raise, *now*. I thought if I kept up with the ache, it wouldn't ambush me.

Shortly after our break, my birthdaughter Rebecca had become a frequent and welcome presence in our home. She provided enormous help and much-needed relief during the transition. And she loved her brothers dearly. The sadness grew duller, and eventually I was often grateful to be, over the next few years, primarily a mother, a worker, a friend.

After supper and baths I would read to the kids before bed, composed and exhausted, anticipating the irresistible fatigue I could finally give in to when they slept. I gave my all to my days and at night, in quiet down time, I refueled. I perfected pasta primavera for one. I watched TV *(my* shows), lulled into a state somewhere between consciousness and sleep, then went alone to bed and read myself into tired-eyed retirement. I got a little fat and was contentedly ensconced in lateral inconsideration. For nearly three years I had no desire to get close and regular with a man. This was my reconstruction period.

When I look back to those years when our family was mending and I was regrouping, there are a few especially restorative experiences that come to mind.

I had always considered the benefits of excursions into the wilderness—camping, hiking, fishing—overrated; I was never really convinced the adventure outweighed the trouble. "Thanks, anyway, but a claw-foot tub is as close to the hinterland as I care to get," I'd say. But for reasons I did not understand then, in the summer after my spring separation from Thomas, I decided we should go on an extended camping trip. I knew next to nothing about tents, mess kits, and portable propane stoves. Nonetheless I bought some gear at our local Kmart and a road atlas and headed out for destinations unknown, with my sons strapped in the back in between blankets, sleeping bags, coolers, and coloring books.

We eased into our voyage by stopping first at a friend's house at the foot of the mountains in Vermont, where our kids picked strawberries, caught and examined turtles, and swam. The next day, with our friends' good wishes, we headed for the border and campgrounds in another country, Canada, never knowing in the morning where we'd end up by evening.

I must've wanted to find out what I could do alone, as the sole overseer of a growing family. If I could drive a semireliable car into a strange place; and if I could protect two small kids at night without helpful neighbors nearby, maybe then I would feel more confident about being in charge of them within the comforts and familiarity of home.

At night when the woods grew dark, after we had washed dishes and hidden our food from wild hungry beasts, we began our before-bed ritual of walking through the grounds, listening for animal sounds, beaming our flashlights into the trees, looking for owls and worse. Occasionally we passed other campers hunched over fires, playing cards, or trying to round up young children. We did this every night, until at least I felt fearless. We rented a boat and took turns, in life jackets, rowing in water over our heads, built fires, and hiked down gorges.

One night a drunken man, who apparently had noticed I was alone with two small kids, came over to our tent and insisted on offering his manly help. At first I froze. Then as he approached our site I inched over in between our uninvited guest and José and James, who were toasting marshmallows. For a minute I had wished there were a man with us—in deep voices with matching large bodies they could've reached a brisk man-to-man understanding. Then again, our woodsy neighbor probably would not have wandered into our campsite had he recognized a head of household, which, in the absence of a man he did not.

As he got nearer my voice got more baritone. "Thanks," I said, feet firmly anchored in the dirt in front of my kids as they sat around the fire, "we're all set. Good night."

Still, the intruder was convinced a woman alone needed his brawny, albeit sloshed, wilderness expertise.

"Thanks anyway, good *night*," I said again. And he finally stumbled away, tripping on twigs and slurring to himself. We put out the fire and crawled inside our tent. I snuggled up close to my kids, wide-eyed most of the night, but feeling, somehow, safer. The bogeyman had paid a visit and I had sent him on his way. The next morning we were on the road again.

On our final day of camping, after we had folded up our tent for the last time, we headed southward for home. We were inexplicably teary. The kids faded in the back seat, both their heads resting on smoke-scented pillows piled between them. I drove on, much calmer than I had felt fifteen days before. The orientation for our family of three was ending, invented on the road, a beginning blessed by fires under the moon, reading books by flashlight in overlapping sleeping bags, zipper to zipper, hikes, swimming in lakes, fishing, waking up in the woods, fresh-air food, our mutual dependence and company. We have a photo album of those days which invariably evokes huge smiles of recognition.

For us, it was a starting point, another chance at family, a fatherless one. The year before had been disrupted by tension and worry. On the road we gathered and tested our team spirit, our ingenuity, and discovered our ability to be happy again.

During this time I became involved in a tenant's group founded to fight real estate moguls who wanted to turn us out of our modest homes. They wanted to scale up our small conjoined apartments in design, cost, and appeal—by adding tennis courts, prohibiting clotheslines, vegetable gardens, and generally ridding our neighborhood of the plentiful signs of family-life mayhem. Fountains were what they wanted, silence, shrubs, tidy decor, instead of kid-strewn, garden-filled, laundry-fluttering yards.

We held meetings (sometimes twice a week) at alternating homes. Mothers, grandmothers, and their children—crying babies, hyper toddlers, patient preadolescents—met and brewed coffee, baked muffins, and dared a plan against the almighty corporation, known to us in the form of two patronizing, gray-suited men with tasseled shoes from New Jersey. Older kids provided child care, everyone made calls, folded notices, and delivered them to residents of our housing units. On Saturdays mothers could be seen walking the routes with their tiny flier-laden active-ettes straggling closely behind. On the days when the media were invited, kids made signs and gave speeches about the homes they wanted to keep. (I have a picture of my youngest son, who in youthful simplicity is wearing a sign he designed that says: HELP STOP THIS NOW.)

Kids love a good cause, especially if it's rooted in their very own grass—the fiery talk, enlivened faces, copious treats, late bedtimes, collective indignation, the righteous unity and hell-bent resolve—and they love seeing their mothers try to turn back the enemy. More important, they are grateful to be invited into the movement, and though eventually our homes were taken, they learned the crucial lesson that trying to rearrange foreboding events feels far better than an acquiescent acceptance of them.

Mothers were mad and kids were empowered. And our families, mostly single-parent households, were fortified by our fight to keep the homes we had made with the riches of spirit despite the deficits of money and fathers.

Like my father, I relied on fables and rituals to provide the linch-pins of our reforming family. The stories we invented were not subject to anyone's alteration, because they resided in the hands-off world of our common imagination. The world outside of our heads had changed enough and seemed, on some days, more ephemeral than our mutual myths.

Monday we went swimming at the Y, Tuesdays, the library, Wednesdays I took for my own and went out with the girls (and have for the past sixteen years), Fridays were Friday Nights Out, which meant McDonald's, the mall, and a TV show until nine. I made up Minnie from Minnieville, who drove a minivan; the kids decided she communicated with our dead cats, one of whom, after he had left the here and now, had found gainful employment in New York City as a security guard. José thought this job brought our late cat great wealth, and he picked up this story each time by imagining, in opulent detail, the cars and houses and Transformers our cat would buy.

On some days, I would find the Magic Bag in the back of my car on the way home from work, which I presented to my sons as found treasure. It contained flashy pencils, clay, or two matching porcelain-handled spaghetti-eating forks, meant especially for two kids on Greenhouse Ave.

When my kids were sick they had the option of becoming King of the Couch, which entitled them to two fluffy pillows, a blanket, indiscriminate TV viewing, and various dispensations, such as foot rubs and juice delivered for the asking. The Special Specialist offered ticklish diagnoses. I was a reluctant nurse, they probably knew this, so they basked in the brief but lavish attention, until the service promptly discontinued and I expected, insisted on really, their spontaneous recovery.

I never imposed the Santa myth on my kids, but James believed, though he never directly declared his faith. I let it be. When he was about nine years old, he drew a picture of Santa diving off a cliff into a sea of sharks, certain to meet his death. He was saying goodbye to St. Nick, a small, once believable story, viable only in the willing soil of a young, unhurried mind.

If I attempted to change plans, the kids became adamant keepers of the schedule. They needed and wanted the rhythm. But as they got older they dismissed, in pieces, our stories as silly and childish, angrily mourning their diminishing innocence. Did they think I thought them dumb enough to still believe in the Magic Bag, or the existence of a geeky character who could communicate with dead cats? They knew I bought that stuff from J. J. Newbury's, they said, all along. They cringed when Minnie was brought up.

I held on longer than they did, easing out, making sure they were ready to let our rituals go, knowing there would be a bit of a free fall, without the religion, into separate, somewhat isolated mental states grown and shaped by their burgeoning individuality.

These frivolous parables along with our unifying sense of purpose and faithful schedule had, at a crucial time, provided a comforting, coalescing haven for our family's regeneration. Within the world of our family we mapped an itinerary, both useful and joyful, in order to move on.

3

Mothers are the maniacs of love.

—PATRICIA SMITH
Boston Globe editorial

There is a passage in Toni Morrison's book, *The Song of Solomon*, in which a mother confronts her daughter's abuser. Pilate, the mother-hero, glimpses through her kitchen window a man threatening her daughter. She swallows the scene, then takes a knife in her hand and moves from the house into the yard, in the slow, precise stride of a tiger stalking her prey. She comes up behind the man, grabs his neck with a steel-strong arm, and with the point of her weapon digs into the skin of his chest. She explains with terrorizing calm that she's not planning to stick it in any deeper, because "it'll go straight through your heart. . . . You can't move an inch cause I might lose control." She promises to release him eventually, but first, she says, "I thought we'd have a little talk." The man begins to sweat.

"Women are foolish, you know, and mamas are the most foolish of all . . . [they] get hurt and nervous when somebody don't like their children. . . . We do the best we can, but we ain't got the strength you men got. That's why it makes us so sad if a grown man start beating on one of us. You know what I mean? . . . I'd hate to push it in more and have your mama feel like I do now. Maybe you can help me. Tell me, what should I do?"

Pilate pulls the knife away after her menacing monologue, which she delivers into the close ear of her daughter's would-be abuser, and he promises never to return. He gazes at the blood on his shirt and runs off without looking back.

When I became the head of my household I worried about changing fuses and dealing with dead cars on winter mornings, but I had always felt I had the necessary emotional gear to protect my family; and surviving the camping trip had, in its way, affirmed that. I had come from a long line of tiger-mothers—there's not a shrinking violet among us. My great-grandmother, Abby Sweat, was a ninety-five-pound matriarch who ruled her family of eleven children with unflinching tenacity. In sepia photos she has a glint in her eye and the wiry spark of a Mammy Yokum. Her husband Seth was a round-bellied, bearded man, who smiles benevolently in the pictures, always standing calmly to the side, seeming to assume that if anything needed doing his Abby would have it done. My grandmother, one of three daughters, said once while we went through her family albums, "Mumma would stand up to anyone who crossed her children. And, 'coss, no one ever did."

My mother, when she was well, took our side without exception. I remember her having firm chilly words with the principal, when the stony Miss Donnegan refused to assign my brother to the sixth-grade teacher my mother was convinced he ought to have. Mr. Galvin was strong in history, and because she knew her son best, my mother argued, she knew this teacher would be right for Clay, who had shown an interest in the same subject. My brother and Mr. Galvin had a very good year.

After my mother's brash display of maternal ire at the beginning of that year, I remember being extra nice to Miss Donnegan so she would think my mother at least had the good sense to bring up agreeable kids (which she had), and had not bred little stubborn monsters in her likeness. My father, I learned later, moved behind the scenes, by quietly making calls to people who could arrange certain requests having to do with our schooling. And he was a polite, conforming presence at parent-teacher conferences.

My grandmother, Abby's daughter Altie Smith, ran everything and everyone with whom she came in contact and was a force to behold. My grandfather was an amiable man with good stories, but he did not like conflict. He would not stand up to his wife (he silently resented her power and his inability to negotiate it), or anyone else who challenged him. His wife headed the Grange, the church choir, was a member of the school board— she saw the direct benefit of this affiliation as having a say in her daughter's schooling—the Eastern Star and the Fire Belles. Her confrontation with a school principal after he had ousted my brother for having long hair is particularly memorable. My grandmother, at seventy and no flower child herself, paid an unannounced visit to the principal, during which she explained in simple, vehement terms that her grandson had a right to make a choice, though it may not have been the principal's, about a hairstyle preference. She bullied the crew-cutted principal into reinstating my brother pronto.

Given her inarguable investment in her community, the fearless encounters she risked on behalf of her family are especially significant. But she did not see her advocacy as a gamble because, it was always clear to us, nothing or no one mattered more than we did, especially in a moment of conflict. That is the simple enduring message.

As far as I knew, pissing people off on behalf of one's children was an occupational hazard of motherhood. It was, by nature, an adversarial job. And I have, in my family's tradition, been a testy warrior when it comes to defending my kids.

Once, when my son and his friends were playing in the street, their ball bounced unluckily against the house of a neighbor. Before I or they knew it, there was a police officer at my door asking if I knew these kids. I looked out beyond the blue shoulder of the law enforcer to see my self-satisfied neighbors peering at the confrontation. I dashed out into the street, the kids and cop following, to confront my neighbor, who I suppose was expecting my apologetic, congenial dissatisfaction with the troublesome kids.

My neighbors started to explain about the ball.

"And you called the cops because of THAT?!!!!" I fumed. "These boys are good kids. They made a mistake. You had kids—were they perfect?" I snarled into their puzzled faces. My son tried to explain and apologize and our neighbor cut him off.

"Don't speak to him that way," I demanded. And then I said that in the future I wanted them to speak to me if they had a problem with my kids. A call to the police, for God's sake, was not necessary. The officer said something neutral, and our neighbors walked away muttering to themselves.

When I got into the house, I slammed the door behind me.

"You do that again and I will personally hang you by your heels," I told my son. "You've GOT to be more careful. Besides, I do not want to have to deal with that neighbor again for any reason. Got it?"

Inside the house he was held accountable—but, in the community, he knew I was and would always be his fire-breathing defender. It's a trancelike state. As they've gotten older and more than capable of their own defense, I still fight the impulse to rush in and grab the metaphorical collars of those who do them wrong. But they have become their own best advocates; so, now, they implore, back off.

How, I wonder, did the myth of the man of the house ever come to be? Because not just in my family but in a majority of the families I know, in terms of sheltering, glue, and effort, the family totems are women—even if there is a man in the house. I have heard stories about mothers threatening nuns, lambasting cops, stopping traffic, and starting movements out of guerrilla love for their kids.

A man can never really know how many children he has, or which ones are his; maybe the anxiety brought on by uncertain paternity drives a man into an arrogant assertion of his superior seat in a family to which he can only be reasonably sure he is related. Thus, in order to cancel doubts about the facts of his family, he declares he will be its ceremonial head, a father figure. (No one talks about mother figures; we belong to an institution.) Father Knew Best because father didn't know—he is beholden to a woman's word to assure *his* legitimacy.

Women risk public embarrassment and personal safety when a member of their family is threatened, endangered, or mistreated—they are fueled by the privilege of biological certitude. More importantly, women are not bound by a respected membership in a community they haven't been welcome in to begin with—so they have little to lose. For mothers, the broad acceptance of strangers (versus the love of family and friends) does not seem to offer a salient payoff.

Men want to make nice in the neighborhood—the fellowship that collectively grants them their hierarchical privilege, that of household chief. Often their preoccupation with guarding their perceived social position overrides real allegiance. When men defend their family it is often because they are fighting to maintain their position as a matter of pride. Saving face, for men, often seems more compelling than emotional loyalty, to one's impulses and to one's own children. When a woman defends her family it is an order from the heart to keep safe at any cost her loved ones, neighborhood standing be damned. Hers is the kind of safekeeping that does not come from ego or bravado; it flows from uncompromised care. And a kid can smell the difference.

Often a woman's instinctual loyalty to those she cares about exceeds the bounds of her motherhood. When I feel wronged and tell it to a man he turns into Sergeant Friday; "Just the facts, ma'am. I need to know all the players," he says, "a graph or some figures, something concrete from which to deduce an accurate ruling." When I appeal to my women friends they say: "Forget about it. You don't need this." They bolt to my side with biased allegiance, whether my position is justified or not. Data have little to do with it.

Men want the whole picture so they don't risk making an error while other people are watching. But, given the scrutiny with which male virtue is judged and the degree to which a man depends on those judgments, it is no wonder he is cautious in proclaiming his affiliations. There is a quote that goes something like: "Women are wiser than men because they know less and understand more." With friendship and families I will always believe it is wiser to realize loyalty than it is to weigh the proof. (Unless, of course, your child's infraction is dangerous to others.)

In a recent front-page story in our Boston newspaper, there was a picture of three mothers, matronly white women, holding pictures of their slain sons. They were delivering personal messages at police headquarters to begin the city's annual gun-buying campaign—a program that buys back guns from people who are willing to relinquish them. These mothers pleaded "to my community, to the nation," on behalf of their murdered sons, in quivering righteous voices for people to turn in their weapons. But there were no fathers beside them on this day.

There is a scene in the movie *Safe Passage* when the mother (Susan Sarandon) literally attacks a killer dog to save her son; and another in which her son is knocked unconscious on the playing field. She, a slight woman, races to rescue him and carries her adolescent son quickly, unflinchingly into the clubhouse. (Her husband seems to suffer temporary blindness when confronted with chaos—the metaphor is hardly subtle.) In both scenes, she breaks several social and safety codes, and acts unwisely, much to the embarrassment and reluctant relief of her son. But he will remember those scenes as moments of consuming love and glory; and as a man he will tell the stories, probably a lot, with humor and pride.

Of all childhood remembrances, scenes of fierce parental advocacy, or the lack thereof, are what stick. They resonate within the chambers of the psyche forever.

Recently my friend Lorraine called and said she was reminded by her son of the time she whacked a police officer with her bag because he was blocking the door to her son's school and refused to let them in.

"I told him I never did anything like that. I couldn't remember it," Lorraine confessed.

"You were blinded by a mother's fury," I said.

She said her son Glen, now twenty-five, reminded her that when he was in the eighth grade there was a security problem and for reasons neither can recall admittance was being denied to some of the students. She had come to school to drop Glen off and he was about to be late. When the cop gave her son a hard time she raced out of her car and approached the entrance, smacked her purse against his chest, and pushed past him with son in tow. The cop, her son said, was stunned, and she proceeded to escort Glen into the school, on time.

"He thought it was great," Lorraine said of her son's proud appreciation for the unforgettable moment.

Anthropologist Margaret Mead said she did not believe in using women for combat, because "females are too fierce." And there have been regrettable displays of a mother's overreaction, such as the woman who shot her son's abuser outside the courthouse, and the cheerleader's mother who plotted the murder of a competitor—this is maternal wrath gone haywire. But such bizarre dramas affirm the might of a mother's furious sheltering, which hovers nervously somewhere between social acceptability and mania.

Fathering, on the other hand, has relied too long on the empty, ego-driven myth of the man of the house. How much easier it is to mimic ceremonial fatherhood—as if, once parenthood hits, a man acquires a patriarchal laurel—rather than to undertake the rugged education, both personal and cultural, necessary to parent any child well.

When José was nine he began changing diapers. Our neighbors, who had recently had a baby, were both parents of older children, and for them the blush of miraculous babyhood had faded. They were tired much of the time. José offered one day to change the infant's diaper when the parents were too busy to attend to what had become an obvious need. They offered money and José, ever the enterprising boy (that year our backyard was covered with cans he collected and hoped to cash in), accepted, at a buck a diaper.

Not long after, he began babysitting. I'm not sure how old he was, but I know he was too young to do it alone, which meant

I had to be there. So I watched over them both, while he, the babysitter in training, read to and played with our tiny neighbor for nearly a year before he went solo. Probably José's incentive to keep our neighbor's son in clean diapers was due as much to a wish to increase his profit margin that year as to his innate comfort with babies. But if offering child care as a chance to earn a disposable income—like shoveling snow, raking leaves, and delivering papers—brings boys to what has been traditionally girls' and eventually women's work, so be it. Both James and José babysat regularly until they discovered the bounty of minimum wage by washing dishes; and entered their teens knowing more about strained carrots and Desitin than I had known when I became a parent, in my late twenties.

If a man's care for his child is a learned ability, if he is one step removed from the immediacy of a mother's surging love, the job of bringing up boys to be men who can and will bring up kids is crucial. We all had better train them early and well.

4

The Widow Douglas, she took me for her son, and allowed she would
civilize me; but it was rough living in the house all the time, considering
how dismal regular and decent the widow was in all her ways;
and so when I couldn't stand it no longer, I lit out . . . and was free
and satisfied.

. . . I reckon I got to light out for the Territory ahead. . . .

—HUCK FINN
in *The Adventures of Huckleberry Finn*

We want to be free; we want to have power; we do not yet want much
to do with responsibility. We have imagined the great and estimable
freedom of boyhood, of which Huck Finn remains the finest spokesman.
But boyhood and bachelorhood have remained
our norms of "liberation. . . ." We have hardly begun to imagine
the coming to responsibility that is the meaning, and the
liberation, of growing up.

—WENDELL BERRY
What Are People For?

Within weeks of being separated from the father of my sons, one
of the first points of order was a sighing statement of fact to my
four- and five-year-old boys. I was about to begin supper after an
especially difficult day of work and called them into the kitchen.
With my hands on hips and their small faces pointed up to my
tired eyes, I announced: "Okay, guys, I can't do this alone. I'm
going to need your help. José, get the saucepan out of the cupboard."

They looked back at their mother in dirty T-shirts through
droopy eyes, said nothing, and slowly moved through the kitchen
to begin what would become the first of many supper-prep col-
laborations.

Previously mothers conspired to keep their boys out of the
kitchen, indeed the house. When mothers interpreted fathers to
their children, they declared a man's work was out of the home,
beyond the place in which family unfolded and closely con-
nected. Even when a man cooked it was beyond the walls—an
event on the patio over the barbee, with an audience. For some
men, there seems to have to be a tangible linkage to ego before
they willingly perform a function for the good of others. It has to
be fun, creative, or publicly acknowledged. To fulfill an invisible
service as part of the weave of daily life, without fanfare and
postmortem deconstruction (which often includes complaining

or self-reverence for having completed the arduous act), too often seems an extrinsic enterprise.

In the past, mothers tended to shield their boys from the tedium and minutiae of daily life, so they could be freed up to think big, eventually joining their fathers in the more important world Outside. Mothers hoped their boys would then duplicate the experience and marry helpmates to pick up where Mom left off, cleaning and arranging the details of their more significant lives. But, unwittingly, women have been purveyors of a most extreme paradox. We enable their unfettered youth, and then complain because our boys become men unaccustomed to fetters.

So it is no wonder that men, after having lit out as boys, return from the Territory reluctantly. What man would want to leave childhood such as it was, and still is in the minds of some men, in a culture that provides an unobligated province for its male youth? With our boys-will-be-boys maxim, we have granted our male children a boundlessly indulgent field of motion (literally), in which, because of their gender, they are free to screw up and do awesomely dumb things in the name of puerile adventure. Boyhood is where endearing slip-ups are interchangeable with nearly illegal acts and bold offenses, and where male kids are exempt from the small, ungratifying work of hemming pants and scrubbing burned spaghetti sauce off pans. With such a free rein in their younger years, we have set up a most generous amnesty for boys; naturally, leaving the playground will cause great consternation.

From the literary boyhoods of Peter Pan, Tom Sawyer, and Huck Finn to the cartoon boyhoods of Dennis the Menace and Hobbs's friend Calvin, boys have been amiably and amusingly permitted their behavioral infractions and heedless antics. In the case of Tom and Huck, their creator Mark Twain became a sour man who bitterly grieved the passing of youth, proclaiming that adulthood (a.k.a. "the damned human race") was highly overrated, confining, and hostile—a veritable insult to the hallowed quest for youthful indifference. And Peter Pan craved an eternal sabbatical from adulthood in never-never land. Ironic that we should call women girls eternally, and are careful to proclaim boys men at the first sprouting of facial hair.

Beyond boyhood, seriousness awaits, where no such re-prieves exist. So-called manhood is sobering, unforgiving, and there is that damn, nagging restraint of accountability—having to consider, beyond the act, how one's mischief may affect signif-icant others. That is the toughest part, it seems, for men—taking the responsibility from which they had been repeatedly absolved in their free-range youth. Adulthood becomes a pesky ordinance in the eyes of a man who fails to see the riches of a fully realized humanity.

And the women living with men seem to be the bearers of the bad news; we deliver the eviction notices—out of the terri-tory before the end of the month or else. It is not pretty work—and has made of me on occasion what would be commonly called a nag. I reject the language, of course, as I do all gender-specific insults. What gives nagging its meaning is a male's disconnected snub. I have never felt nagged; and have rarely if at all heard other women complain about it. And that is probably because we make a connection, for better or worse, before the third appeal. (For example, "Yes, I heard you. No, I don't want to do that.") A woman who is nagging is a person who hasn't yet received the connection she craves. So she repeats herself. It bounces off him; it appears she hasn't been heard. She says it again. He's riled because he has in fact heard it but he wants not to. He says she's a henpecking shrew, because he wants to be released back into the wild of his adolescence, and it's a female's insistent words that keep him from going there—in peace, anyway.

Those of us, usually women, who plead accountability ap-pear as background cacophony to be outwitted, silenced, or defied. We are always and forever the spirit-dampening Aunt Polly to their free-wheeling Huck.

I, for one, take no pleasure in being an omnipresent irritant. I persist because I have a vested interest in sharing the drudgery. I want to go float on a raft too, say to hell with the fence for a day or two, light out and get "free and satisfied." And I keep thinking, Why can't males see that if they assumed more of the little work we'd be less inclined to be their carping fun-busters, more inclined to help build the raft and float with them? Or at least happily grant them a guilt-free bon voyage.

Ever aware of the inclination of males to run free from minutiae (and even more accustomed to the begrudging tendency of my gender to scoop up the resulting unattended messes), I made it a point to share the details with my sons and to delegate tasks with adamant persistence. That meant die-hard training through a fundamental rhythm achieved by repetition. When my sons would say, "Get off my back," or "Stop nagging," I didn't. I rephrased what I wanted to be heard, *after* I told them I ha-a-a-ated those words. I heard it as the battle cries of soldiers tenaciously guarding their ample reserves of immaturity. Increasingly, their I'm-trying-not-to-hear-that attitudes became so inflammatory, and I reacted with such venom, that they seemed to prefer my harping reminders over my ire. Eventually, they paused before speaking, and then switched to unisex rejoinders, such as "Chill," if I itemized their incompleted kitchen tasks. I loathed being told to freeze my discontent just as much. Or, behold the miracle, they averted my subsequent requests by picking up their socks instead. Then they got funny.

My chore jones became a family joke, represented in particular by my son's drawings—he used art to editorialize much of his dissatisfaction—of Helga the Choremaster, a leather-clad whip-wielding dominatrix with gritted teeth and an uncanny resemblance to his mother, which he posted on the kitchen cabinet. Helga had big balloons over her head in which José quoted some of my most often heard orders, give or take an embellishment or two. A short while later, he produced another picture, of a woman with a hideously wrinkled visage bordered by unruly strands of hair, and eyes pitifully frozen in contempt. He titled this, simply, Mom at 50. Cute.

Yeah, I'm thinking, that's me after twenty years of ceaseless grumbling. Maybe this is why women enter middle age looking and feeling less sexy than they ought to; and men glide into elder dignity unscathed. Women are Aunt Polly-ed out by the time we've raised the kids and managed the house for a decade or two; we are the sum of our scornful reminding and our detail-plagued lives. Behind every suavely graying man is a woman whose roots have been dyed and pulled out on a regular basis. What I want to say, when he posts his unflattering cartoon, is: "Yeah, that looks like the woman I might become if you don't learn to pick up after yourself. In the name of aesthetics, make it not happen."

Some days I persevered more than others, and over the years they reverted to all of the above, with diminishing regularity and mixed results, but always aware of the dynamic.

What fueled me on the better days to keep pushing was the memory of my time in the childhood labor camp that was my parents' house. I did not like the exhaustive list of chores back then; on the other hand, I do not recall feeling tortured. I remember waddling to the clothesline with a plastic bin full of heavy damp clothes at an age so young I could not easily reach the ropes above. When we were young, my brother and I were valiant workers; we washed dishes and clothes, ironed, vacuumed, and made our own lunches from the second grade on. When my brother became a father, he was for many years a househusband, the primary cook, and launderer. He kept track of

everyone's keys and mail, separated whites from colors, and did
the grocery shopping. Though his organizational skills have been
valued by his family, I think he may have grown as weary as I of
the drudgery. But as adults I know we both have often looked
back to our childhood regimen as a privilege few kids get—a
hasty affirmation of capableness.

I am sure that the teaching of manners and delegating
chores have, more or less, the same goal in mind—to bring
slowly but firmly to our children (who begin life as immediate-
gratification-seeking, infantile egocentrics) the recognition of
other forces in the universe besides Self. When a child says thank
you, excuse me, or please, he is forced, at least by the moment it
takes to utter the words, to consider others. Chores and manners
take on new and essential meaning for teenagers. For however
long it takes to fold the towels the adolescent is drawn out of the
embryonic self-absorption to which, by this age, he has returned.
Besides, I supposed, if they did these things for themselves—
ironing, cooking, cleaning—then doing them for someone else
might not feel like such a stretch. It might even become a reflex.

I was so committed to raising sons who would not presume
that females everywhere should jump into action every time a
male's appetites grew or needs were not met, I became an anti-
service, self-reliance zealot. I may have made issues where issues
may not have been.

When my sons were around nine and ten, a wise friend,
Elizabeth, suggested another perspective. For instance, she said,
if I made my kids' lunch every now and then I would be giving
them a part of me to take to school, a small warm reminder of
their mother's generosity. Okay, so I could be, ah . . . kind, a
quality not diametrically opposed to my wholeness or theirs. If,
by making a sandwich and wrapping up some cookies, they'd
know I was thinking of them, I knew I wanted that. I started for

the first time to occasionally pack lunches and pick up socks without feeling oppressed.

Providing services for them did not mean I would turn into a martyred dishrag of a mother; and it did not mean that they would grow up considering women nothing more than suffering servers. Bringing them juice or ironing a shirt only meant I wanted to help them out, and that I hoped they'd want to help me out too. (Though I confess I can count on one hand the number of times I actually ironed a boy's shirt—by the time they were old enough to care about wrinkled clothes, they had been unalterably programmed not to expect that *I* would press them.) But it is the earlier Helga years, I am convinced, that inspires them to say thanks just about every time I do what is generally known as women's work for them. The presumption was removed.

As surely as mothers and fathers endorse the undomesticated free-wheeling of boys by withholding realistic previews of adult life, they shelter their daughters from the opportunistic aggression of boys. ("I know what they're capable of," a father jokes with caution, "I was one once. . . .") The solution, I think, is to allow girls a broader, looser sense of independence and to shore up a boy's presumption of the same; to encourage our girls to *take the space,* and to remind our boys to relinquish some of theirs. It's a turf issue, a kind of social colonialism which boys have felt entitled to and girls have been made to feel unqualified for.

Adventure is good, when infused with lessons in compassion and responsibility. The Ajax is in the cupboard; when you're done, go play, get nuts. If, as parents, we can suggest to our boys an adulthood that is gradually subsequent to and not incompatible with their boyhoods, then maybe as men they will not flinch when eying maturity. Maybe.

The increase in working mothers (especially if they are the only parent) means boys are being pulled back into the house, not only for practical reasons, but because a boy belongs in front of the sink as much as his sister and mother do. Working mothers cannot do it all. Sons are getting to know their kitchens, their dirty bathrooms, the best brands of laundry detergent; they are seeing, in realistic doses, a doable adulthood.

5

Without a father, he may never become a man.

—FRANK PITTMAN, M.D.
Man Enough

That woman keep families together, by now, can hardly be argued. (Often to a fault, for better or worse, as evidenced by the current language—enablers and facilitators—used to describe our overgiving.) And in terms of financial support, while there are many men who are providing for their families (I live with a man who helps support two), more women than men, apparently, are doing it alone.

In the latter part of the twentieth century women have taken on more responsibilities, and men have lost, in the reformation, a recognition of and commitment to their essential obligations. The public perception of manless mothers (women, it is suggested, who had wanton sex with a transient man and then went right on ahead and had that love child) as a jumbo drain on tax dollars is quirky, ludicrous, and just plain false. The mothers are not the drain, the fathers who are not paying are. What brings our attention to the soaring number of mother-run families is the appeal to the public to help support kids whose fathers will not. A paying father can erase a statistic.

"Without us," the male media thunder, "you and the little ones are doomed to be miserably poor and deprived," suggesting that single mothers, who have at least by definition remained with their children, are to blame for the negligent fathers. Men keep defecting, women continue to be implicated for the fractured families left behind.

Whenever I hear the term "broken family," I am reminded of a line in the TV series "Grace Under Fire," uttered by the strong-spirited single mother played by Brett Butler. When she visits her son's school, the condescending teacher begins by saying, "I understand [your son] comes from a broken family. . . ." To which Grace replies something like, "No, our family is not broken. It was, but I fixed it."

In *The End of Manhood*, John Stoltenberg writes, "Millions of mothers raising children today are being unjustifiably faulted if there is not a carrier of manhood in the home. But nothing about a child's secure sense of selfhood . . . depends developmentally upon the strictures of the manhood act. Absolutely nothing. . . . 'Single' mothers they're often called. Singular is more to the point."

Single mothers, generally speaking, are a strong bunch—they have to be—but they are not yet possessed of super powers which will turn men into responsible parents. In 1997 we are still blaming and bashing our mothers not only for what they have failed to do but for what the fathers refuse to do as well.

Perhaps fathers are paralyzed by ambivalence during the revision of their familial value, having to share a title—head of household—that was once exclusively theirs. If we are expected to endow, they reason, then we ought to at least have a prominent place in the kingdom; or, if we cannot be all, we will be nothing at all, and so they head off the playing field altogether, sour and rejected.

Yet, it seems, women have not abandoned their traditional duties while hurtling full force into *their* revised roles. Women are and have been doing men's work without fanfare for years now; we have entered the work force in large, assertive droves, are feeding ourselves and our children, and have entered politics and the military (inasmuch as anyone should) with notable and growing success. But, the research has it, we are still doing most of the cooking and child rearing.

Louis Farrakhan, head of the Nation of Islam, zealously urges the return of black males to their positions as family leaders; and in so doing united hundreds of thousands of black men for the Million Man March on the capital in the summer of 1995. (I could not resist thinking that if each man present pitched in two bucks the child support debt could have been significantly reduced—but they filled the coffers for the Islamic cause instead.) It is unfortunate that perhaps the most forceful (though regrettably askew) idea to come forth regarding the crisis in fatherlessness is being endorsed by an anti-Semitic, misogynistic, homophobic racist. Sad too that his approach, ultimately, is both naive and impractical. Fathers can't expect to return to families as if kings out of exile, and expect to rule the women and children who have been running the house.

Promisekeepers, an immense and tightly organized association of Christian men who meet in stadiums, is the tamer, more middle-American version of Farrakhan's man-as-head-of-household remedy. Their credo includes reverent, retrograde promises to protect and cherish their wives, and to return to a hero's baronial headquarters in their families once again—Ward Cleaver with a virtuous vengeance.

What is it with these guys and their groups? Something happens to men when they meet en masse; they get dizzy. Gen-

der-based gatherings are good for the short term—a crowd's
power can be contagious and acts as a springboard for personal
activism. For women, certainly, groups were good for a while.
After years of having been isolated in their respective homes,
women came out and found mutual strength and collective wisdom. But men have been conglomerating and making unified
decisions all along—there have always been thousands of kinds
of exclusive fraternal organizations. The group is not what they
need; diluting is what's been missing. It seems the clannishness,
not the cause, becomes the identity of their all-male associa-
tions—what rises to the top is clarified testosterone. Now even
women are nearing a time when our groupness may be getting
tedious and mushy; we will begin to repeat ourselves and lead
with our gender, when I don't believe that was ever the hope. For
bands of men, the time has come for dispersement into the ranks
of a general population.

Not too long ago, a letter from a member of the Coalition
for the Preservation of Fatherhood appeared in my local newspaper. The letter writer was miffed by a recent editorial that eluci-
dated the dreary details of this year's domestic abuse casualties.
The man—I'll call him Ed—wrote that the number of female
deaths had remained constant, but the number of male deaths
had drastically increased. I read the same editorial, and what Ed
missed is that the rise in men murdered was the direct result of
abusers killing not just their ex-partners but their girlfriends' or
wives' new boyfriends and children (three sons had been included
in the body count); apparently perpetrators have begun to take a
more comprehensive retaliatory approach. Ed then writes that
while domestic abuse can "sometimes be tragic" it was just another crime, "not a pressing social issue." Moreover, he didn't
like that the editorial was "criminalizing general segments of the
population." Men, for instance.

Call me daffy, but I just can't think of a situation in which domestic abuse is not tragic. And no one is picking on men here. They are criminalizing themselves because they are over-represented as transgressors in the crime of domestic murder; snuffing out your ex is illegal. Most unsettling is that the letter is from a member of an organization of *fathers*. With this man's cavalier dismissal of a growing, desperately heinous crime against women, one can only shiver at the thought of the kind of tenets his group holds dear. Ed is trying to make a case for his gender; but, by annihilating the opposition (and the facts) with an appalling lack of common sense and sensitivity, he misses all the points with hideous consistency. Did Ed always feel this way, or did he get dimwitted when he got caught in the heady current of his club's mobilization? I for one am left believing that men should not gather in groups of more than two (this includes football games), unless they are supervised by a professional who is certifiably enlightened; otherwise they feed on their own toxins, get wacky, and go blind.

This is what these mass movements don't get: that, for the good of all, men must learn to adapt to a *division* of labor, as coproviders and coprotectors. And that women don't need adoration and a reinstatement of our secondary roles, we need peers. Like bumbling well-meaning warriors, these men, armed and eager à la Keystone cops, rush off to fight the enemy, only they're headed in the wrong direction. *Sharing authority* is the deal, but men do not seem to come easily to this.

While men are busy actualizing their paternal worth, single mothers are busy bringing up their families and should not believe nor should they be made to believe that *they* are the nasty statistic in a foreboding trend. We should be telling single parents they CAN do it, not that they are any less a family because they are the only parent who is trying to do it.

Assumptions about the honor of men in families have disintegrated before me in sober and certain order, leaving me to question whether the requests we've made of men were unfair and unachievable to begin with. Certainly our expectation was not based on inherent talent. Who then imposed the legend? The women who believed the creation of father-champion was what a family needed; or the men who weren't about to walk away from a hero's welcome? Or both?

Are women who have more children than they can responsibly support or care for depending on—subconsciously—the elusive father icon to make their partial families whole and secure? And are men overwhelmed by the call to honor?

If men and women agree to debunk the impossible demands upon which we have historically based fatherhood, if we grant men a cooperative presence *within* their families, will they, can they, respond with loving parity?

What I see in the teenage sons of single mothers often fills me with an intoxicating optimism. Not because I prefer a fatherless family, but because I see mother-run families as an intermediate condition that can contribute to the greater effort to create workable families, headed by adults, eventually both female and male.

In the nineties, women and their children are being left by the baby-boomer men whose fathers were *emotionally* absent and whose mothers sanctioned their flight from home. The result is an increasing number of fatherless households, granting mothers a greater breadth of expression and parental jurisdiction with their sons than they've ever had. Most would have us believe that these mother-reigning homes (twenty-four percent of the nation's families) are the beginning of the end of family, including the mothers themselves—many of whom believe, with guilt, the male-deprivation myth.

I have wrestled with the meaning of my children's fatherlessness for the past twelve years, while remaining defiantly committed to raising boys whose confidence will supersede the so-called deprivation. I know well that the retreat of a parent hurts, but I remain ruthlessly optimistic. Once when responding to a man's concern about his ability to be a good father without having had a close relationship with his own, José responded by saying, "I don't worry about that. Maybe I'll be more like a mother as a father."

Mothers are training their boys to know and express their feelings, not because we insist on turning our sons into males manqué whom we wish to coopt in our bitter grudge against their gender, as some members of the men's movement would argue, but simply and obviously because no one else is doing the job—and the job must be done.

Too, the girls of their generation (for whom the trail was blazed by mothers of the women's movement) are having their say, and a visible effect on their male peers. My sons' female friends know tae kwon do, drive fast cars, play basketball, take dares, and call boys—many of whom might have been labeled tomboys or worse in an earlier era.

Both mothers and their sons are reinventing family. It's a work in progress. And while laws insuring the rights of children and women are critical, the decisive work, the real revolution, must occur within our families. With self-knowledge comes enlightenment; a humane morality will follow.

Part 5

Boys

*A mother is not a person to lean on, but a person
to make leaning unnecessary.*

—DOROTHY CANFIELD FISHER

1

When my sons, around the age of twelve, approached puberty, they lowered the gate. This part of my life, they announced, the chapter coming up involving girls, possibly kissing and the like—I will *not* be sharing with you. During this time I absolutely could not say the word "sex" without them cringing and huffing. When they began to sort out their sexuality, they would cleave a chasm between us, grappling for some certitude or focus in an otherwise foggy passage.

They were, in their ingenuous way, gratifyingly firm, businesslike even, in qualifying the course of our connection in the upcoming years. As my mother had with my brother when he was eight and she refused his kiss, they were enforcing our severance, per order of the culture. While fading out of their youth and jolting into uncertain adulthood, their boyish clarity on the subject of mother-son communication, oddly, comforted me. Still, for a time, I felt banned from the world of their hearts.

When they were about nine or ten I remember consciously grieving over the passing of their sweet feet, of the small androgynous bodies I could carry on my hip, hold on my lap, when affection was simple, spontaneous, and not loaded with gender and individuation issues. But for a while I felt I ought to back away from gushing hugs and motherly smooches, grant them the distance they seemed to need to search and separate. I waited for their cues.

One time when James was meticulously latching the gate, he softened his lockout by saying, "When I'm about nineteen or twenty, then we'll talk. I'll probably be telling you about my girlfriends then," when he'd have this romance thing sorted out. Now, though, he seemed to be saying, "A boy's got to be a boy and, like other frontiersmen my age, I will forge the territory motherlessly. Eventually," he promises with a tip of the hat, "I'll be back."

When my birthdaughter was adolescent we talked about her progressively broader tours outside the home—from dances to boys' cars, and bigger decisions. When she was adolescent, we had difficulties, but topic-censoring was not among them.

Boys give up a lot to be men. During their preteen years, on the cusp of manhood, my sons began leaving behind gender-ambivalent tendencies: tears, dancing, sewing, lap sitting, and seeking their mother's confidence. Daughters get the social nod to stay the path with their mothers; they're expected to continue to be close. Though it is often a ragged and trying nearness, a girl and her mother can enjoy an uninterrupted tie without doubts being cast upon a daughter's blooming womanhood. (The saying goes something like: A boy is a son until he takes a wife; a girl is a daughter for all of her life.) But male children have to be more careful; if they are viewed by their male peers as being suspiciously bound to their female parent, they collect names which are meant to question their imminent manhood. I've heard "MB"—Mother's Boy—used derisively by other boys to describe a son who acts as if his mother matters to him. Being called a Mother's Girl or Father's Daughter does not suggest the same lack of character in a growing kid.

There seems to be an unspoken sociocultural suggestion that the extent to which a male is attached to the women in his life, first his mother and then a wife, is the degree to which his masculinity remains in question; as if the very closeness to the other gender corrupts his ability to master his own.

But as my sons gained momentum on their testosterone-fueled trek to adulthood, they intermittently retrieved most of the things they did and enjoyed before masculinity was the goal. Gradually they rediscovered and picked up old activities, like so many lost socks in the confused mess that is their rooms. Soon they resumed dancing with a vengeance (they couldn't stand not to), my oldest son took up sewing again, reconstructing straight-legged jeans into retro bell bottoms; and they would flop onto my lap, occasionally, if only to show how implausible it is for a six-foot teenager to sit on the knees of his five-foot-four parent.

Shadowy mustaches, deep voices, and the consistent attention of girls had granted them enough equity in virility to allow them a return to what would've previously been considered, before the visible presence of hormones, a few iffy activities.

When I noticed that a few of James's nails were shiny, he was unfazed. Nothing much was at stake.

"Nice polish you got there," I said, smiling.

"Think so?" he said, undaunted, undefensive, at ease in his female friend's sheer nail enamel. (She had asked for a volunteer for sampling.)

Many years before, when he was not entirely sure of his gender, James was not so blasé about his looks. When he was a baby and for years after, people would comment on how beautiful his eyes were, "and those lashes, what a pretty little girl," they would say; or "What a waste," they would coo, when I said he was a boy. So when he was six he disappeared into our bathroom and emerged with suspiciously unadorned eyes. Having grown weary and frustrated with the attention his flashy eyes seemed to draw and the consistently incorrect perception of his gender, he stepped up onto the commode, and with his face close in to the mirror, clipped off his lashes with his child-sized scissors. I was shattered. I went into the bathroom and found his elegant little lashes in a tiny furry pile in the sink. He was unrepentant. I said I hoped they would grow back, quickly.

But as they confronted and passed through puberty, they became more relaxed, even playful, with their appearances. José and James were, through their teen years, platinum, reddish, two-toned, bald, close-cropped, and shaggy; at one time they both had earrings. They had discovered their alterable features—and seemed to vary their looks as a matter of amusement or impulse.

I do not think I would have been as pleased with a girl who wanted to do same, given the pervasive cultural messages that what they look like is not good enough, should be rearranged or enhanced for reasons less than playful. With my birthdaughter Rebecca, I urged her to keep her wiry curls intact, emphasizing her natural beauty and stressing the significant preemption of her nonphysical appeal. The difference in mothering sons and daughters seems to be a constant awareness of equilibrating the impact of cultural checks and balances of the gender kind.

Though I welcomed a boy's long-due comfort with cosmetic play (the kind girls have always had), I drew the line when it came to facial mutilation. When James was fifteen and wanted to pierce his eyebrow, I found myself delivering a righteous sermon about the face, his face, his father and I had made together in love; why would he want to perforate our naturally pleasing creation? I surprised myself with the evangelical tone of my plea. I framed my disapproval of his desire to mar his face as a personal affront to the people who gave him life, who drew up the plans, whose features were represented and which were lovingly blended in his. Overwhelmed, he left the room without debating the issue. Later I heard him tell his brother that he had planned to have an eyebrow ring but "Mom went ape."

When they were thirteen and fourteen, aside from liberating their looks and reviving their unisex activities, they were still not ready to resume the heart exchange they had had with their mother when they were young. Which, in many ways, was fine . . . and normal.

I know the intimacy of a mother's love can throw a man-boy off, especially during the hormonal murkiness of teenagehood. A mother's sheltering love can confuse both a parent and her child as she tries to figure out her new choreography during the drama of her son's necessary separation. I could not follow my sons around town, keeping fast cars, cigarettes, and bad pills out of their reach. It would not have been comfortable for any of us if I had, out of devotion and worry, interrogated them about the details of their secret lateral lives. Another way of loving them to death had to be invented.

At first, when my sons stepped away, I kept trying to remind myself that their exoduses were not personal (though I was reminded that much of my behavior was dorky); that my place in their lives (the female authority) and an overriding social mandate enforced their detachment. Though I always felt they were dying to talk but thought they were not supposed to. (Who told them not to? Why?) I became convinced that humor counts for a lot. And faith.

I was comforted during this time, for instance, that my boys had never stopped hugging and kissing their mother. I took that as their tribute to the kind of unconditional closeness that comes from living our lives together, the sort that makes us able to read, without words, each other's souls; the kind that cannot be unhinged by peer disapproval.

Sometimes their affection was oblique, like when James would lumber down the stairs in his boxers, first thing in the morning, half awake, and come over to me as I sipped coffee and read the paper.

"Good morning," I'd say.

He would wrap my neck up in his arms and say, "Half nelson, try to get out."

"No," I'd say, calmly, half annoyed. Still it's contact. During this dicey segue, they seemed to be saying, "Bear in mind my love." Then, while they withheld their personal stories, they offered the best they had—their goofy but heartfelt filial embraces.

Until our reconciliation, in a manner of closeness designed for a man and his mom, we circled each other, tentatively, lovingly, deferring to and informed by a society's idea of masculinization en famille.

Still, I cannot help but wonder whether, if a boy did not feel that he must pry himself so completely, and it seems unnaturally, from his mother, he might not feel the need, as a man, to transform a wife into the mother he was forced to leave. If a boy can continue—beyond his essential individuation—to be close with his mother, as a man he may see women as individuals, not as resurrections of a once lost, blunted, and unconditionally loving connection.

2

*Both boys and girls need a male mother as much
as they need a female mother.*

—JUNE STEPHENSON
Men Are Not Cost-Effective

After they had passed through puberty and emerged on the other
side—firmly entrenched in teenagehood—my sons began fulfilling every possible cliché about repugnant teenagers a third-rate
Catskills comic could contrive. Ba-da boom.

I finally figured out that it's okay to hate fifteen-year-old
human behavior.

They can be loathsome and they know it, and are secretly
appalled if we are not. Because appalling is the plan. They want
to shock us into casting them out, thus expediting and easing
them in their awkward, ambivalent acts of separation. If we indulge their world-class self-absorption, indefensible displays of
contempt, and tedious melodramas, they are likely to lose all
perspective whatsoever. It's up to us to gaze at them in disbelief
to remind them of real-world emotions. Such glib utterances as:
"Excuse me." or "You're kidding, right?" can provide useful con-
text for the unscrupulous teen. Also, it is important to understand that who they are now they will not be; fifteen-year-old
human beings are a rough, exploratory draft of the people
they will become. At this time, it is also comforting to recall all
the stories we've heard and the biographies we've read about
acclaimed geniuses who, when young, were incorrigible, nonconforming underachievers . . . like Einstein, who flunked phys-
ics, and Thoreau, who did jail time.

And while we are letting them go, it might help to repeat: "Okay, okay, you are no longer my little honey bunny. You're big, huge in fact, you don't need me, I don't worry or care about you anymore, you know everything there is to know, I know next to nothing aside from dangerous facts and how to make you feel guilty and bad. Go, my son." Which is what they want to do: go. When they are not begging for attention.

Their morphing into manhood seemed too often like watching baby chicks breaking through hostile jagged shells, emerging wet, overwhelmed, solitary, and dazed. And they crash through and retreat ten times a day. My adolescent kids seemed, alternately, to want close company and help and ample personal space in which to stretch and figure out if they were going crazy.

The smallest request becomes the most invasive, oppressive demand. There is a collision of revisions in the adolescent—a logjam of self-images not wholly centered, grounded, or definite. With the burden of quick-changing bodies, and a rigorous rear-rangement of life views (Am I my mother's son? Or am I my own man? Not quite. If not, then what?) a metamorphosing kid can be threatened by next to nothing, and quite often nothing. He is operating at peak frustration by just *being;* so it takes a mere hint of an inquiry to push him off the plank. Incidental propositions translate into intolerable strife.

A simple request from a parent, such as "Pick up your towel," seems to undergo a perverse translation in the adolescent mind. He hears: "Sweetie, I'd like you to sandblast the Acropolis before you hit the books, and tomorrow before school? Count the dust bunnies in the attic, and arrange by size."

Our parental perceptions get rearranged in the battle, too; our standards sink to bleak depths and we latch onto any effort on their part to communicate, anything, at any time. We cling to whatever promising glances they seem to behold of a future (i.e., beyond the next two hours), life subsequent to immediate fun. In addition, as the mother of kids whose gender has been characteristically discomfited by close encounters, I was easily seduced by their attempts at what sounded like meaningful conversation, no matter how slight.

My younger son used the word "stress" a lot to refer to normal life occurrences, such as schoolwork and the usual parental concern. So now we have given teenagers a word for their hormone-induced angst, as if it is a condition we must heed, lest we cause them great harm.

In the midst of his strained separating, James and I had a dinner date—a check-in because he was out of the house so much. Most of the talking was done in the car—a perfect setting for teenage-parent dialogue; they can't go anywhere, and we the drivers can't make concentrated eye contact, thus allowing them to say to the windshield what they might not divulge to a fully alert parent. I said I wanted to know how he was (and basically who he was); and he said he hated when I worried. I stated as dispassionately as I could that I wanted to get him safely through teenagehood. "Then you have nothing to worry about," he said. "I make good choices."

"But there are dangers over which you may have no control."

"Yeah," he explained, "but your worrying doesn't help. It stresses me out."

On our way home I said, "What then will be our agreement?"

"We don't need an agreement," he said, "we need an understanding."

At first, I was impressed by his response. What I had generally thought to be the male take, that no conversation should begin much less end without the guarantee of a certifiable point or remedy, was mine. The request for connection was his.

"Okay," I said, "you're right."

But really what we needed was an agreement, a quantifiable, repeatable plan; not some telekinetic, floating mind hug. There are times when talk is cheap and connection is extraneous. In my experience, men do this well, and kids, especially teenagers who are fraught with emotion to begin with, can benefit from a parent's cool impassivity. Sometimes a deal is just a deal, bare and immovable.

In the early years when their father lived with us, I remember asking my two- and three-year-old sons what they wanted for supper; they had a choice—soup or chicken. Thomas took me aside and firmly confided that we were not running a restaurant. We would decide what supper would be; they would eat it or go without. At first I thought his approach was chilly, unkind; but I have since seen the merit in ipso facto authority when it comes to kids who are simply too young to practice the privilege of choice in their own affairs.

Over the past forty years the hierarchy of the American family has shifted from the 1950s Parental Autocracy when fathers knew best through the '60s Parents-and-Kids-as-Roommates Motif (Can I write on the walls? Whatever) into the Child-Centered Ensemble of the 1990s. This latest incarnation includes a cast of thousands—beginning with but not limited to the Parents as People in Waiting and includes extended relatives, neighbors, anyone who is privileged to share the aura of the child in question.

I have seen a toddler lead the way into a coffee shop with his posse of child-pleasers trailing behind, and for the duration he is granted the jurisdiction and clout of visiting royalty. (Maybe it was my WASP-ish restraint, but when I took my

toddlers to restaurants I practiced fiendish inconspicuousness.)
The party of four is led to a table by three-year-old Nicholas.
After he decides he'll sit on a big chair (having rejected a lap and
the booster seat), all chairs are positioned to face the child.
When he bemoans, loudly, the yukky taste of his cheese Danish
(which he insisted on having), everyone at the table starts tearing
off pieces of their pastries, as if they are the king's men eager to
find their majesty's pleasure.

A three-year-old should not have to be plagued with this
kind of decision making so early in the day, so soon in his life.
There'll be plenty of time to exercise his options; and the best
instruction is to show him how by choosing for him. At three
years old, Nicholas is not ready. And besides, that's what parents
are for—to share the wisdom of their seasoned rationale.

In my early motherhood I watched the men around me
with their children, and I remember being both distressed by and
in awe of their detached guidance. My brother would issue orders to his crying child, seemingly unaffected by the tears that
bored holes in my heart. He would coolly continue with the
intended plan. "Pick up your toys and go to bed," he'd say, as if
he were reciting the date. And Thomas, in addition to his strict
kitchen protocol, seemed unmoved when our obviously unhappy
children did not want to wear the clothes he put on them. I
would think: How is it possible not to feel his despair as your
own? I could feel the ache in *my* throat when one of my young
sons fought back tears. Supersonic empathy took over, and would
inevitably water down my resolve. I began thinking there was
sound reasoning in the concept of having both male and female
parents present. And now I think it is even better for all parents
to embody both.

When I became a single parent, I began slowly to practice
fathering. Unlike the men I'd seen who seemed to be able to
summon instant unsympathetic control, I had to pause first to

disconnect my reactive impulse before I could follow through with conviction. Eventually I realized my children could not only survive but often benefit from my dispassionate supervision, though when I erred it was always on the soft side. (A fact, nevertheless, I do not regret.)

After James had convinced me to settle for an understanding, I felt duped. I had been boomeranged by my own agenda, of wanting my son to embrace the female within. So what if my worry stressed him out? I'll use what I got. It is not a bad thing to be affected by the fears of loved ones. So while I'm basking in this boy's barrier-breaking pursuit of togetherness, he stays uncommitted, out of the woods, off the hook. This is the fallout of mothers who try hard to bring up sons with a talent for talk and sympathetic bargaining we saw too rarely in the men before them. Our overcorrection and their new-found, fearless wrangling skills get us where it hurts, in our power differential. We agreed he'd check in; and that I'd try to develop a hardy, blind faith in him and his teenaged elusiveness. And I got even more male in the parenting department.

Sometimes I resorted to the lavishly blunt (therapeutically incorrect) non-"I" statement, such as "You are being a jerk," instead of: "*I* feel concerned and anxious when you behave in a way that feels jerkish to me." A kid is the first one to know when he's being revolting, and a parent's tame robotic response can render the adult a fool in the eyes of the savvy teen. I cannot think of parental pandering without remembering a most daunting scene that took place years ago and the small child of a friend smashed me in the face with his tiny dirty hand. "Faces are not for hitting, Zachary," she said, admonishing him matter-of-factly. Great, I thought, she's instructing him in the uses of other people's faces, and I'm fighting an urge to bind his little hands into a Houdini knot. The kid, both contemptuous and wily, sneered at his mother and smiled spookily at me.

But really, I admired then and still do James's urge for clarity, that it is the route he chooses when there is a pressing conflict. He wants the air cleared; he finds comfort not in chasing away tension but in uprooting it for all to see. The alternative—backing away and burying the clash—is not his inclination. I saw it in him when he was young; and I have seen undiluted empathy in dozens of other boys—their friends, my brother, our friends. It was THERE—the sympathizing spirit that usually gets shamed into submission, perverted by social expectation, or bullied by other boys and girls.

When James was eight he wrote and illustrated a story about a ball player who discovers his baseball is alive and has feelings. Ouch, it hurts being hit, the little boy hears. When he strikes out, he insists that what matters is not the score but the source of the pain. He writes: "I didn't care. I just had to find out what that noise was." He finally figures out that the baseball is being hurt, so he takes it home, asks its name, offers it something to eat, and then takes it to the park. At the end of the story they are cozily leaning against each other in closely arranged stick chairs, with an understanding. "When we go to the game, he is my good luck ball," he writes. "I would not want him to say 'ouch' again." The end.

Like most small boys, José and James talked freely about hurts and sadness and anger. I saw every time they childishly trashed someone as a cue to mention compassion, or another view. And I found myself thinking: You CAN take it with you; hold on to that tenderness, keep talking (and listening). Stay with me on this, the payoff is large, and it feels good, too. Trust me, there's something big in it for you.

The hardest part was preadolescence . . . the time when hormones arrive and take no prisoners, when gender is ruthlessly tested for questionable slippages into the other side. I thought, perhaps subconsciously, If I can make them believe that their instincts are redeemable in the world at large, just as manners are, and that their natural-born inclinations can provide enormous equity in the spheres in which they eventually hope to travel, they will want to keep and mine their early tendencies to communicate.

Not a year too soon, not a moment overdue, girls started paying attention to them because, they said, they listened and talked, without judgment; and thus it was, alas, reinforced by the larger world, the most attractive segment for them at least. Reinforcements from the male sector would not come as easily.

Nevertheless, after our meaningful car talk about his angst and my concern, and the ultimately flighty cure to both, I took a turn for the concrete, and reinforced my father side. We still sought an understanding to resolve significant disputes, but James's curfews got nonnegotiable, I got more imperial, and when he would ask if he could have three kids sleep over, I said no; and the reason? Because. Just because.

3

Academia was another adventure altogether.

The unpleasant little truth is that José and James do not respect authority. They are the Question-Authority generation's exemplary but irritating bumper crop with a vengeance. Sometimes, they respect people who have authority, but power in the abstract does not seem to move them.

From the very beginning of their public school careers my sons have failed, for the most part, to find purpose in the arbitrary format and seemingly aimless requests of classroom learning. When I was a student, especially in elementary school, I appraised the challenges before me, prevailed, and received approval. I got A's. But I have said many times that I didn't begin to learn or think until I got my first C—in tenth grade, at an elite public all-girls high school where discussion and individual opinions were not only encouraged but expected. My brief visit to coed public high school was a dismal detour in cerebral listlessness; the teachers did not seem to care about what I thought or knew, they just wanted the boys to behave and for everyone else to observe the rules and linear goals. Not that conventional academic merit in the mandatory years in and of itself is not laudable. But it is what it is—task mastering; and gratefully there are more than enough students who value and aspire to that format—but my sons are not among them. I have been reminded of the words of Mark Twain—"I never let my schooling interfere with my education"—many times throughout my kids' bumpy tour through the educational system.

Preschool was a breeze. José cheerfully shaped Play-Doh, he loved to sing, dig dirt, and glue things; he appreciated his snacks and could sleep anywhere. But by the second month of kindergarten (read: systematized learning, his teacher laminated everything . . .) I received the first of what I began to refer to as the October Call. He wouldn't keep his shoes on, they said, he had trouble "attending," he made big messes and asked too many questions. In his mind, like my brother years before, the particulars of his six-and-a-half-hour classroom education seemed to pale when compared with the parallel study hall of his imagination.

José saw hibiscus and toucans in the oaks outside the window while everyone else was doing multiples of three; he pondered words and collected their meanings while others were piecing together small mimeographed sentences (in second grade one of his many tests revealed he had the vocabulary of an eighth grader). José's preferred reading included *Ranger Rick* from cover to cover, encyclopedias, maps, and almanacs; he stockpiled knowledge the way some kids amassed Legos. By the second grade, he seemed to think his logic was equal if not superior to that of some of his teachers. That being the case, he reasoned, why should he listen to and conform to deficient instruction? He was not difficult or ornery; he simply drifted.

For the existential student, every rule, conflict, decision, and directive becomes a Goliath-size inner discourse and search for salience. Without the gear to accept the perfunctory, José spent his schooldays trying and more often than not failing to find purpose in his academia. It was no wonder he was tuckered out by recess and nearly comatose by noon.

For thirteen years of tests, October Calls, and teacher conferences, José remained a dedicated, creative resident of his head, with brief ambivalent appearances in the classrooms of his formal schooling, where he felt forever off key and out of season. (Alas, he got enough intermittent A's to carry him past the rugged patches to the end.) In his senior year (God in heaven, I thought it'd never come), José continued to experience an overriding simultaneous out-of-school education. "I know it's important to you that I do well in school and I will, but the experiences I'm having now . . ." he explained as he exhaled with a sigh bloated with revelations. He was referring to the deep discoveries of relationships, romance, responsibility, friends, adulthood—all of which he felt he had to confront with full consciousness and immersion, thus compromising any engagement he might be expected to have in his anatomy and physiology assignments. So, he declared, his schoolwork might suffer. I was thrilled he ventured sensitively and thoughtfully into terrain so many males barely consider, but, I advised him, "It may surprise you that most people do not call in sick while attempting to live the examined life." He would have to study both, the mandibular *and* human discovery, if he hoped ever to exit the institution of which he was so uncomfortably a member.

José and James, from their earliest years, were made aware of and involved in causes and movements beyond the personal. We went to anti-nuke marches and demonstrations, and spent time in the library afterward, reading books and looking at pictures that would both explain the threat and soothe their fears. When he was ten, José and I slept on a cold bus during a ten-hour overnight trip to the capital to march on Washington for reproductive rights. After an earlier suspicion about the actual event of abortion (he was still too close to the occurrence, chronologically), he was as outraged as a ten-year-old could be that anyone would actually try to tell someone what to do with her own body. He made posters (which he wore), and walked miles among noisy, exuberant demonstrators. And when we were in D.C., José and I visited and lingered in front of the Vietnam Memorial, where he stood silently and sadly, trying to make real his father's experience.

I was no political zealot; but I was committed to introducing injustice and agitation to my kids from the start. I have since deduced that the ways in which I have encouraged my kids— questioning the status quo, forming opinions with a righteous, self-confident regard for justice in all things—do not effectively interface with the public school experience. And I have paid dearly, with time and explanations and apologies and frustration and meetings and phone calls and groundings.

The boys? They are not passive aggressive. They are not passive anything. They don't know how to surf over a perceived outrage (no matter how tiny) into nonvocal compliance; they are unfit to ride out any inner or outer conflict. If they venture into what seems a compromise of their true essence and philosophical bearings, they think they will awake screaming in the night, mere yielding fools, haunted by ghosts of apathy past.

For instance, in the eighth grade José refused to stand for the pledge of allegiance. After having studied American history, he said he believed, as the settlers had, in separation of church and state, and was opposed to the "under God" part. I was called to the school. His red-faced teacher, a patriotic man, said he would not tolerate José's defiance. All of his students, the teacher seethed, were required to stand out of respect for those who believed in the pledge. José solemnly suggested that others in the class might want to sit out of respect for his equally worthy belief. His teacher looked as if he would combust. I asked if there was actually a rule on the books requiring a student to stand and the vice-principal said she was sure there was, would get back to me, but never did. So José quietly left the room during the pledge for the remainder of the year.

My early and longstanding admiration for the movie *Ferris Bueller's Day Off*—which I took my kids to see when it first came out and which we have rented several times since, about a boy who circumvents the school system with spirited inventiveness—could've been interpreted by my kids as a kind of training film, I suppose. They can quote whole conversations between the principal, the bumbling Mr. Rooney, and Ferris, with perfect comedic inflection. The premise does not exactly inspire a pro forma reverence for the daily constraints of traditional classrooms and controlling teachers.

When I complain to friends about a son's most recent act of defiance, they look at me askew, as though I have missed the obvious explanation. "I wonder where they got *that* from," Merrill says in mock amazement. Okay, so I don't abide authoritarian fiends sweetly. For instance, I am unwisely—childishly—intolerant of arrogant police officers. I am not proud of this; and I know that in the long run it is self-defeating. I almost always get traffic tickets, when they might've been avoided, because I am incapable of affecting what feels like a fake deference for a

man who struts to my car, places his dark blue crotch and holster
at eye level outside my window, and grunts orders. I can respect
the man past the uniform, a humane enforcer, but I cannot and
do not want to be expected to take seriously men who get their
authority only from badges, guns, ranks, and getups. Pulleeeeeze,
I always feel the urge to say (and foolishly sometimes do), "Get a
job. Don't bring that haughty police act over here . . . go arrest
my neighbor, for crissakes, who crawls into his car every Friday
night after the eighth beer and drives dangerously home." (My
sons, ironically, caution me against my usual attitude in these
matters and are far more respectful of officers than I.) Now
firefighters—Lord, they come as close to the meaning of hero as
I can imagine.

So when my kids complain with fire in their bellies about
their unjust, autocratic teachers, explaining it's hard to settle and
silently accept what are to them trifling directives, I pause. I say,
choose your battles; I say, keep your indignation, don't get cynical, but figure out what's expected and just, damn it, do it. I say,
get through the year, breathe deeply, and say nothing.

When my youngest son told me about his teacher who
threatened him by yelling: "If you were my kid you'd be on the
floor. You will respect me!!!"; and my son answered calmly, "No,
I don't have to respect you. But I will try to treat you respectfully," I was *mortified* and said, "You MUST treat him with respect." I'm also thinking, Jesus, I wouldn't want that brazen little
shit in my class (but really I've always been partial to upstarts).
But what I wanted to say is that the threat of corporal punish-
ment is unnecessary, that, right, people earn respect. But I say,
Be silent and follow the godforsaken rules. Halfheartedly.

With teachers who encouraged thinking, discussion, and were
passionate about their work, James and José were without excep-

tion responsive and succeeded. But I bounce around. My Yankee ethic tells me, Of course you do well when you're having a good time; master the difficult and dull—that's where character is found. And then there's my indulgence of the spirit, which asks, Why the hell does learning have to be such an adversarial, unimaginative boot camp?

I am still unsure how their infuriating disregard for theoretical authority and petty rules will translate into adulthood. They both were active in causes in high school. José worked diligently with an organization called the Peace and Justice Corps throughout his senior year, which included visits to inner city schools to try to resolve violence, racism, and abuse. On one occasion José's approach to one school's struggle with gang conflicts was to make and put up posters which stated simply, NC LOVES HOODS, and vice versa. And James was a founding member of the Diversity Team at his high school.

Teens in general have an ardent dedication to fairness, roused by a slow, mean dawning that nothing, really, is fair. They rage into that good night, one last plea—in their voices is the cadence of one daring the evident. Think of the revolutions, both quiet and passionate, high schools could ignite with a teenager's raw righteousness and energy. Instead, they are asked to be quiet, sit still, and write neatly. High school is often a regrettable waste of youthful zest.

One of their stepfather David's and my favorite teacher conference moments involved a history instructor who proclaimed, "The problem with James is he likes to communicate."

David and I exchanged dumbfounded stares, and with confused inquiry, David said, ". . . Ah, he *doesn't* like to communicate . . . you mean?"

"He asks too many questions," she said, stolid in her disapproval.

"And . . . ?" I said.

"He has an opinion about everything," she said, with obtuse self-satisfaction. "And my classroom is not the place for it."

But I wonder: Are my dreaded trips to the school the price I pay for the men I wanted my sons to be? Have I breathed into them my despair about retreating males; and have they inhaled my hope for them to be different? Or have they inherited the best of the man I fell in love with, the empathetic activism I saw in their father in the early years? Is their gawky diffidence a manly authority in progress, awaiting refinement?

In my more cynical moments, I considered their awkward navigation of institutional learning the inability of males to master multiple concepts. Throughout their school years they may have felt they had to be passionate individualists or thriving students; but not both. On the other hand, José has been the one among friends to call the ambulance and prevail with unflinching concern during teenage emergencies. He has hauled sick bodies and cleaned up messes; he has provided urgently needed care and selfless attention at *all* of the times that it mattered.

Some of the time their youthful reflexes have been untimely and dumb, fiascos in which they reacted with annoying recalcitrance, without sense or relevance. But I know they are and always will be people I want close by at my crises. They jump into action and take quick, smart control; they rise like wildly plumed phoenixes, fueled by their furious good will. *They respond.* They have become the men who wouldn't think twice, who don't think at all before staring down the clash and confidently staying the course.

Some days I just felt like a bad parent of two insolent brats; maybe I didn't espouse the value of fitting in enough, of going along; I wonder whether I should've instilled a slight but useful fear of one's elders, or at least a reasonable reverence for the symbolic. Maybe I could've made their lives easier. Other days I thought I should've promoted reticence and a career in accounting. But there is no discernible shy gene or math ability in our family tree, so the chances it would've taken are slim.

My brother and I were raised to believe that one must earn one's floor space—that is, be there, participate. This was a blend of my father's evident high-energy effort to be ever charming and my mother's often stated wish to have her children feel at home in the world—she wanted us to believe that the globe was as much ours as anyone's. Personally, I have always felt that shy people suffer from delusions of grandeur; they envision the rapt attention of everyone present. Ever since the first grade when Alice Moulton would contract into a ball of pain if the teacher called on her, and the class would come to a long, labored halt while she was cajoled into uncurling and speaking at least one soft word, so we could get on with our lessons. I find myself wanting to say to the skittish introvert: "Trust me, no one is paying as much attention to you as you fear they are. Get over yourself and pitch in." So it is likely, had José or James shown tendencies toward inhibition, it would have been intolerantly coached out of them. Then again, perhaps they could've learned selective repression.

When José was in the eleventh grade, I started my countdown. I vowed that when he graduated from high school I would dance on the tables. *"Muchas* merengue moves, José, I'm not kidding. On the table tops, blitzed out of my mind, when that day comes." He knew I'd never get drunk, never had, but he was amused by the idea, and had a true feel for the relief his academic closure would bring his beleaguered mother.

When that day came, he had finished with atypical A's, a final, celebratory surge. As we walked to his graduation, with his long black shiny robe billowing in the wind behind him, he looked both chic and humble, more manly than ever—a finished boy. I dissolved into tears when they called his name and he stepped onto the stage. At the party afterward, he said the di-

ploma was as much mine as his. A generous touch since I had
not received one of my own, and I wept some more. But then I
could not stop grinning; we the women, the mothers of teens,
discoed in the dim-lit kitchen way past midnight with merry,
provocative abandon, as the men and boys, both admiring and
outshone, shifted uneasily in their chairs.

In an essay about freedom of speech in the workplace, Bar-
bara Ehrenreich defends the critical spirit and believes "suck-ups
make lousy citizens." I'm hoping. If nothing else, I know I look
forward to the day when both my sons' lives are wholly their own
to explain and I no longer have to answer for their contrary ways
and principled disobedience. It's exhausting.

4

The years after teenagers discover Life Apart From Parent, and
before they are willing to communicate any of it, are shaky. They
seem to be silently, precariously treading behind an impenetrable
reef, divvying up values, their own, their parents', their peers',
those of the community at large—and deciding which ones they
want to keep. During this time we think our kids are younger
than they are and they are sure they are far more capable than
they actually can be, given simple chronology. We haven't caught
up to their rapid growth, and they have glimpsed adulthood and
they think, prematurely, it is them.

Unfortunately, parents and teens are operating with inaccu-
rate databases, skewed perceptions, and unreliable communication when all of the above is desperately needed—during the
onset of cars, drugs, drinking, and sex. My friend Merrill calls it
the Age of Peril, a silent, aching vigil, informed by persistent fear

and intractable faith. It is the last blast before legal liberty—when parents, forced into the scenery by our beseeching kids, are trying to see and not be seen. When I once asked a coworker, Eleanor Murphy, how she survived bringing up three teenage boys by herself, she said: "I worry to a point and then give the rest over to God." I have thought of her words a hundred times since, because it is true, if we don't check our worry, it will travel to the haunting ends of the earth and we will surely go mad. When I began to feel choked by the tugging ties that bind, I would practice a prayerful detachment.

For me, it was not easy to stop asking who, what, where, when questions—of the minor kind. Sometimes I would pause mid-sentence, knowing I had stepped on my sons' autonomy, realizing I was looking for answers I didn't really need or have a right to. It is an exercise in forced passivity that does not come easily to those of us who are inclined to assert and who have a tendency to take over when we think we smell trouble around our loved ones. As much as we want to save their day, we are reminded we cannot carry, explain, retrieve, or reroute them. *That* time has passed. We are done with the teaching; by now our values, for better or worse, should be emblazoned on their brains. When I launched into one of my dozens of tenets regarding teenage activities, James would cut me off and drone, "I kno-o-o-o-ow how you feel," and then he'd finish my sentence exactly the way I would have and had dozens of times before. And I'd say: "That's rude," but think secretly, Ah, sweet affirmation, he's been listening.

You chant to yourself, Please, God, just let them get through this day without doing much damage to themselves and others. Bless their random acts of adventure, anoint them with life assurance and outrageous good luck. Keep all incoming calls from being the Bad One.

When I stayed up until 11 P.M. one night waiting for James

to return home from the first night of his summer job, he said, "You didn't have to do that. It's only a job." And when I dropped off José at the bus station to go back to school and waited for him, as I always have, to board, be locked in and on his way, I saw him wave me off from my rearview mirror. When I didn't go, he approached the car.

"Mum," he said with smiling condescension, taking my hand in both of his, "you simply must let go. You *must.*"

I smiled back and said, "I know. I know," and crept in my car up to the traffic light and left him behind.

Which is what the mothers of sons must do. We remain quiet except for the occasional strong and loving word (the satellite disconnects after about three and a half minutes anyway). We clasp our hands, and stay still and steady so they can hunt for their alleged manhood.

Part 6

Guys

1

This part begins with a book about a pig. I got a call at work one afternoon from James's first-grade teacher. She was concerned. He was not yet reading and it was the middle of the year; she wanted to test him, to see why.

"No tests," I said firmly. José, who preferred daydreaming and drawing, had been tested ad nauseam, with nothing much revealed other than that he preferred daydreaming and drawing.

I did not want my youngest son to be studied by specialists or examined for anything. Besides, I had faith. I knew he'd be reading soon.

"Well," the teacher sighed, "if he's not reading by the end of April vacation . . ."

"No tests," I said again, thanked her for her concern, and hung up the phone.

Two weeks after April vacation, I was sitting on the sofa in the living room when James came blasting through the door after school.

"Mom, Mom, listen to this." He crawled up onto the couch, his legs still too short to bend, with his sneakered feet jutting out past the seat cushions. He held a book in his lap, and he began to read. He'd study a page, and work his way through the words, then look up at me and beam, searching my face for approval. I smiled back, elated, relieved. The book, *Pig Pig Rides,* was about a boy pig who learns to explore and exert his independence, and by the last page his mother is warning him to be careful as he rides proudly off. Her son, Pig Pig, asks why, and she answers, "Because I love you." That simple. But, oh, it was true, and at that moment, after James had successfully read through a book whose words had finally made sense, I was a tearful fool full of motherly pride.

A year later, David McPhail, the author of the book James read first, was the guest speaker at a young authors' conference to be held at a local school. Both José and James had books on display at the conference, as did Merrill's son, so we had planned on attending. Having dashed out of the office, I came into the auditorium late and found the seat Merrill had saved (she had transported our kids to the event). After arranging myself as unobtrusively as possible, I looked up and was instantly entranced.

"I'm in love," I whispered to Merrill within minutes of seeing the author.

This is what I saw: a tall, genial, confident man. Gentle. Funny. Sexy. Calm. A man comfortable in his skin, loose-hipped. Generous. I saw towering patience. No pretensions, at ease with the young squirming kids in the front row. I saw his yellow sweater under his brown wool jacket, I saw his fluid hands. I saw a man so fine I was sure he was out of bounds, out of mine anyway.

I imagined he'd be a man who would like long-legged, silky blondes who wore nothing but natural fibers, and whose ancestors had done something quietly historic, such as found a museum or discover a gene. But why would I be attracted to a man whose tastes would be so different than the appeal of me—not tall, dark-haired, a cotton wearer for sure, but utterly descended from underachievers? The outside chance. I had hoped, dreamed maybe, that he would be more than the sum of his visible refinement—that the hint of a lusty defiance I thought I saw in him was true.

And I liked that he had work. I have never thought of a man's success as an aphrodisiac, but I found McPhail's achievement in his chosen field very appealing. Here was a man who was not striving, or knee deep in angst on an ambivalent path; he had a realized livelihood for which he had gained obvious recognition. This time, when I had become eligible for romance I was a mother in my mid-thirties, and as a result had become fiercely precise about what kind of man I was willing to live with. Whatever tendency I may have had to rescue, nourish, or upgrade a man had disappeared—I was doing all of that for my children: pricey guys were out. I was supporting myself and my children, had good friends, fulfilling work, and there appeared to be no reason to be with a man other than my extreme passion for him; and of course his secure acceptance of my priority—my kids. I wasn't about to forfeit the solitude for which I had paid dearly, for a mediocre and/or draining love affair. I had a life, wanted, needed, to keep it, and could not spare large amounts of intimate social work to feed a workable duo.

At the end of the presentation we walked into the lobby, everyone buzzing about how "accessible" the author seemed to be—that was the word one adoring teacher used. In the lobby I joined a long line of autograph seekers. After about a half hour I edged up to the table and handed him my book. He smiled, then kept his eyes on the page and never looked up.

Over the next several weeks I thought of the man more than once. At the time I was an editor of a lifestyle magazine, and McPhail was a resident of the state. James, who was seven, must've sensed my interest. He suggested I do a story on the author. Hmmmm . . .

I contacted him over the phone, he generously agreed to be written about, but two days prior to the interview I got nervous and tried calling my brother, who had been writing for the magazine, to see if he would do the interview instead. No answer. I had no choice.

At twelve o'clock on a Wednesday afternoon I arrived at the small country store at the foot of the mountain where he was renting a house for the summer. McPhail had asked me to call him so he could show me the way up the narrow road to his house. When he arrived in his red car, and gracefully lifted himself out of his seat, I swooned for the second time, and noticed, in the July sun, that he had the face of a man still open to joy. His blue eyes were clean, easy, unhurried. Over lunch (he had made sandwiches for us), in between interview questions and answers, we talked about kids, schools, relationships, art. By the time we had moved out on the porch into the breathtaking view of the mountains, he was asking about me, my work. He was refreshingly free of self-importance. He listened.

At the end of what turned into a daylong interview, he said he didn't know my personal situation, but would I like to have dinner sometime.

I said I would like that very much. Then I got in my car and trembled.

A week later I wrote him a letter in which I said I had lost my editorial distance, that I was putting someone else on the story, would he mind being interviewed all over again. No, that'd be fine. The next time I saw him, we kissed on the beach, he held me close while moonlit waves lapped the edge of my skirt. That was nearly a decade ago, and he has been in rich, frequent doses all that I felt he would be when I first saw him. And more.

In the three years after my separation from Thomas and before I had met David, I had decided to spare my children the temporary, uncertain company of the men with whom I occasionally spent time. I didn't want them to have to fret about, imagine, or begin to forge a connection with a man for whom I felt anything less than what I was reasonably sure would be an enduring love. After about a month of knowing David, I was sure. And David knew from the start I came with kids. That meant our relationship would eventually spawn two others; between my sons and the man I loved.

2

A stepfather is a circumstantial relative. The children and the man are brought together because of a woman's love for both. Not because of the kids' and the man's mutual love for one another, and often despite it. This choice, they want it known, was not theirs. Problems seem inevitable.

When my oldest son was introduced to David for the first time, when he was nine, he walked past him into the other room; blatantly and rudely dismissing him. He refused to look at, much less shake the hand offered him by, the man who he thought was trying to be his father's fill-in. What followed was a tumultuous three-year showdown, which included direct and indirect insults, ambushes, and rejections. He would hide David's shoes when he was about to go out, ignore him when he spoke, and disrupt the mealtimes that were so important to David and which he insisted, through it all, in maintaining, without much success. José knew then as he does now that even as a young boy he was a formidable presence, both clever and imposing.

But David stayed patient. Most admirably he never forfeited his adulthood to do small battle with the boy. He never judged, labeled, threatened, or competed with him, which my son will never forget. And David never tried to be Dad.

In the first couple of years I would get frustrated with David when he backed away from being authoritarian with the kids. "Take a hard line," I would say. But he balked. "I can't do that," he'd explain perfunctorily. "They know and I know I am not their parent. How come you're the only one in this house who doesn't know that?" So he settled somewhere between being an uncle, a guardian, and a friend—a stepfather. Later I heard Dr. Spock talking about stepparenthood, from his own experience and subsequent professional opinion. He advised: "The first thing to know is that you cannot nor should you try to act like a parent to your stepchildren." He said he had tried to govern his stepdaughter, and it had been a nearly irreparable mistake. After backing off, he said, they were finally close. David and my kids seemed to know from the start what took Dr. Spock and me longer to figure out: that a stepparent is not a parent; and that his position in the family he enters is best forged with kindness and distant charge.

One night during their third year of living together, José and David were moving wordlessly through the kitchen. My son slid into a chair, as David prepared food at the stove. José spoke to David's back with gritted teeth. "There's not enough room for both of us here," he mumbled in his most convincing Wild West adolescent voice. David dropped everything and went over to him, placed his hands flat on the table, looked into the boy's big-talking eyes, and announced softly but firmly, "I'm in love with your mother and I'm going nowhere."

It may suggest hyperbole to say that since that man-to-boy

gaze in the kitchen my son has shed his hostility and replaced it with love and appreciation for his stepfather. But that is exactly what happened. José was ready to give it up; he was issuing a final, halfhearted challenge, and he seemed, finally, to be convinced that he could back down and get out of the duel without paying a king's ransom or losing face. David had made that clear in a dozen different ways.

Since then, they have shared art supplies, dinners for two, and long talks about mothers, brothers, and UFOs. A few birthdays back, José drew a picture for his stepfather—a large outstretched hand, against trees, and profiles of calm people in green and blue borders with a verse that began: ". . . to one of the few purely good and kind people . . ." Finally, they are together somewhere beyond the childhood battle and mutual adulthood.

My youngest son seemed to accept David's presence from the beginning. Maybe it was the pig book, or James's merry uncritical nature that carried him through the early years with the man his mother chose. Certainly David made it easy. During the seven years James played baseball, David was there for all but two and a half games. Once, after David had driven three hours to attend his own son's game (he usually spent the night rather than make the trip back the same day), he returned, sprinting to a seat beside me in the stands, to catch the final three innings of James's game. When he arrived he didn't complain about the hot traffic and the six hours he was confined to his car, but simply said, "How's he doing? Any hits?"

David has been capable of gargantuan acts of selflessness throughout, such as picking up his stepson in the middle of the night hours away because the boy missed the last bus. Or sitting patiently forever in a doctor's office with a coughing kid, or waiting up at night for the Return of the Teen. He has accompanied me on trips to the school to explain, advocate, and resolve academic concerns on behalf of his stepsons. He cooks the kids' favorite meals; he makes sure they have warm jackets and boots in the winter; and sketch pads and pencils when we go on vacation. He carried my youngest son up to bed on his back for years, until both of them were too old for the haul. And David did this all without expecting anything except knowing he was there for the kids; he has never reminded me of the time and care he's given his stepchildren, not once.

Meanwhile, David has respectfully left a place in our family for their missing father; he would not presume to step there. He knows he can't fit. My older son and David silently guard this place together, so they understand, as much as they respect and love one another, they can only get so close, given the empty seat between them. My sons have relied on the support and shelter that two adults provide, on the unyielding faith of a loving man and the viscous threats, nagging worry, and doubled-up protectiveness of their mother. While in our house, they could only safely consider themselves the children of one parent and the stepchildren of another.

For over half their lives David has given the best of what he can to my sons; he has loved their mother well. They love him for that, for being there, and for reasons they've yet to know. He has always accepted, without self-congratulatory claims of sacrifice, that a family existed before he arrived. So he defers to the intimate dynamics of us three, alternately amused, impressed, and overwhelmed, while remaining constant in his support of us all—and of his own four children.

But what David has brought, among many things, to my children and me, to our crumpled and aching ideas of fatherhood, is an unfamiliar vision of grace—he has been a believer, a supporter, a patient adult man both responsible and humane. I never really knew what a father did, how he was supposed to act, but I, and my kids, now know we have seen it.

3

I am now with a man I expect to love for the rest of my life. He is like my father in many ways—they shared an affection for the romance of baseball (and an endless fund of related trivia), and my father possessed an amiable gentility, as David does. During the last years of Sam's life, David became a good friend to him—when he visited he'd read to him, take him for walks, and for long dinners at their favorite restaurant. David, who is tall and inclined to hug, provided my father with a protective affection he so desperately missed as an old man, impaired and alone. When he hadn't seen David for a week or two, my father asked for and about him with an enthusiasm which had all but slipped away in the last few years of his life.

But the man I love is different from my father in ways that make it possible for me to live with him; he is generous in all things, is a world-class listener, and expresses unwavering faith in all that is me. My son, in reviewing my pattern of affection for non-WASP men, once declared with ironic sincerity, "You've finally settled down with one of your own." And I have. We are compatible in the extreme.

More than any other man, and as much as I could fairly expect, David has encouraged me to loosen my taut rigging and sail free. Though selling the sailing idea and behaving in a way that makes it plausible are two very different concepts. He, for one, lives for fun; thus casting me, at times, as the disciplined compensator (two dedicated fun-seekers are not likely to get the bills paid on time and remember all the appointments).

Recently I realized I liked very much being called to a waiting supper and asked David if he'd be willing to prepare dinner half the week (he had been cooking once or twice weekly). Sure, he said, jolly and agreeable. The first day, he left his studio on the third floor at 2 P.M., went on his Euro-shop expedition, which means he bought a baguette here, some fresh fish there, produce at a local farm, some wine, etc., buying half of what we had already and which I had shopped for with coupons and purchased on sale. Then he planned and prepared, with drawn-out and laborious detail, the meal. It was truly painful to observe the lack of efficiency in time, money, and execution. I said I wasn't sure it'd work if he planned on presenting a Martha Stewart meal half the week.

"It's fun," he countered. "I like doing it this way."

And then I say, "It doesn't have to be fun every time you cook. People have to eat even if *you* are not having fun."

"Oh, I should be serious, or bored? If I can make it fun, why not?"

When he says this I feel prudish and think of H. L. Mencken's definition of Puritanism: "The haunting fear that someone, somewhere may be happy."

It's painful to watch, I say. And given the intensive labor and high production costs, when finally seated for dinner I often feel like an honored guest at an anticipated premiere, instead of a family member at a meal. The buildup is burdensome.

"Don't watch," he says.

"I won't. I can't."

Aside from his costly and time-consuming amusements, David persists in cheering me on into levity, while providing the most solid sustenance I could imagine in a man. He does not take for himself what he would not be willing to recommend, freely and often to me. Adventures are mine for the asking.

Within a month of knowing him, I had a chance to go out with friends one night but had no babysitter. He offered to watch the kids. "Oh no," I said, "I can't let you do that." He insisted. "Let it go," he said, and those words fell warmly and deeply into my tightly managed heart. If we women want the men in our lives to share the oppressive duties, we surely and absolutely must let it go, even if we're pretty sure they won't pick it up and do it our way. So I went.

4

Men occasionally stumble over the truth, but most of them pick themselves up and hurry off as if nothing had happened.

—WINSTON CHURCHILL

In my loving relationship I am reminded still of the glaring disparities between men and women. Mostly it has to do with what I call the I-frame (I as in ego; frame as in encasement).

It is where some men seem to fitfully reside. Its walls are made of tender armor. When his frame is threatened, challenged, or endangered the man inside responds as if the house is coming down; he acts as if his fortress is being stormed, and, feeling unarmed, he fights to keep his shelter intact. Inordinate confidence and courage are required in order to believe it won't; to come out and connect, despite the threat. Opening the door and exposing himself to his contenders—emotions and intimacy—indicates a man's willingness to take on the fright of wholeness, unsheltered by his cumbersome housing. And only then can he know that his perceived rivals are not his enemies at all. It's kind of a Catch-22. He's got to leave the frame to find out he doesn't need it. Even with the most warmhearted men, men I have loved, I have seen the I-frame.

An example. Recently I went to my sewing room to finish a

quilt. But my machine would not go on, and the lights would not work. I changed bulbs, I checked the circuit breaker. Finally I announced to David that there was no electricity in my room. "The power is out in the whole house," he said. "Why didn't you tell me?" I said, miffed that it had not occurred to him to share the info. He had been on his own parallel search for the reason and forgot to include me. But he saw me trying to sew, yes? He got steamed. "It's not my fault the power is out," he said in defense of himself. I was not blaming him for the power outage, I said. Please, I was thinking, step out of your I-frame, and come near and hear what I'm saying. This is not a personal attack. I just would've liked to know, is all. This is not about you versus me, or your inability to solve the problem. He stood at the doorway and listened in pain. He left, after having endured my appeal. And I-framing is not characteristic of the man I know. These aberrational displays of ill-adapted egoism appear as a kind of hormone-driven petit mal, or at best, evolutionary residue.

That is, the world is not and has not been for several centuries now a place where men must be prepared to flaunt their plumes and competence, and kick the undomesticated butts of male rivals in order to win and keep a female's attentions. They needn't show they can provide shelter, many acres, and lots of moolah (women are doing that for themselves now) to prove that they are, among all other men, the man for us. There is next to no need for a man to be ever alert to primordial threats—we are out of the wilderness, the Industrial Age has come and gone, and we are all, females and males, floating through the cyber frontier, where I-frames are of little use, save for our threatened anonymity. So it is safe to come out now.

———

Some men are willing to jiggle the latch on their tightly guarded autonomy, but they do so with edgy humor. They are not entirely convinced they want to step out, so they keep one foot in the fort and one foot dangling precariously, teasingly, on the ground outside.

I noted this tendency when I started perusing men's magazines at the gym to relieve the inexpressible tedium that is the Stairmaster. (Reading material was limited to a months-old, sweat-stained pile of tattered muscle, men's health, and money mags.) I read the first-person columns first; I wanted to know what men were saying about themselves, but after about the third article I was frustrated with what seemed a pattern of the essayist's unfinished notions. The writers were content to leave their essay-sized observations merrily unresolved.

The defeated yet amused smirk male humorists affected when joshing about the limitations of their gender felt a bit too restless. They sounded like the nervously sad relative at a funeral who keeps telling jokes to the truly grieving mourners, hoping they'll laugh their way out of their woe to join him in his jovial denial. It's funny, it's true, it's really true, it's really funny, and ummm . . . The guffawing subsides, the room grows darker, gets quiet, and becomes drenched in a pall of anxious ache and bewilderment. Then the joker slithers away from the funereal gathering and disappears.

There seems to be an abundance of males more than willing, in print anyway, to take a soft look at their historically bound and socially driven behavior. Like the easygoing English teacher who wrote about turning into a savagely insensitive, hat-throwing, cursing, dirt-kicking primate when he took a job as coach of his small private school's football team. He realizes he's turning into his worst memory of his boyhood coach, the crusty beast who wouldn't allow his aspiring athletes to drink water after playing in the heat for hours, and referred to the gasping dehydrated boys as "ladies." The writer of this piece gets fired eventually from his athletic duties. But the teacher cum retro-coach does not deliberate long or deep enough to figure out how he could have avoided the reflexive instinct to become an ass when drilling boys. He doesn't discover or at least does not share any newfound knowledge about how to be a mentor with hu-mane authority. Worse, he doesn't seem to want to. He sees resolution in just not doing it. He gives up coaching for good, sticks with teaching, and is a happy man. The end.

The writer of another column explained he was too embar-rassed to tell his son that boys have a penis and that girls have a vagina. So, in the absence of physiologically accurate parent-provided info, his son makes up his own names for genitalia (an animal in the case of his own, and something sounding like exotic pasta for the female equivalent). What happened to the good old days, laments the uptight father, when bio-lore, albeit misguided, was available on the proverbial street corner? He solves his dilemma not by forcing the uneasy words out of his mouth for the benefit of his kid's honest education, but by in-dulging his son's anatomical misnomers and hoping he'll eventu-ally find the facts the same way he did, from someone other than his dad. The father doesn't even want to reschedule the antsy discussion for another time, when he thinks he might be able to pull himself together long enough to deliver the data. Hardy-har-har.

An attempt to Know Thyself is laudable, all the better to find purpose and direction. These writers of maleness know themselves all right, and they laugh at who they are, but they dispose of the resulting wisdom like a soiled diaper. I want to hear how these guys resolve such conflicts, how they move through and beyond the potholes of useless (and hazardous) masculinity to get to the other side. Okay, so he turned into a toxic goober when he was in charge of a bunch of boys with a pigskin, then what? So he was flustered by the P-word and the V-word, but he reconciled his humiliation with his fatherly duty, how? What about the insight racked up as a result of this gender-driven turmoil? Where are the remedies? As the mother of boys, I can use the lessons of these fathers. But they exit the circle before it closes. I think these writers, in the words of essayist James Thurber, "stick to short accounts of their misadventures because they never get so deep into them that they feel they can't get out."

Encountering one's reflection, especially if it's distorted, can be a truckload of giggles. But taking a restive look at the absurd man in the mirror is not enough. Finding resolve beyond the image, before signing off, doesn't have to sober up the chortling crowd; enlightenment can be hilarious *and* inspiring. Besides, if these guys just keep chuckling, boys will keep referring to penises and vaginas as Mr. Pickle and Miss Winkie or, worse, they'll internalize the dirty unspeakable of what exists "down there"; and men will keep coaching boys into shame and submission, who will then become *their* worst reminder of what a coach is supposed to be, and so on.

I'm all for the rallying power of humor during rugged confrontations with self; it gets us past the glaring looking glass. But when the chuckling dies down, it's time for movement. Otherwise the multitude of acutely daffy gender tendencies gets hauled, via self-knowing snickers, into the next generation. Funny. Very funny.

Maybe men keep laughing because they are terrified of what they might uproot if they burrow in the depths.

Not long ago I shared a dinner with David and a friend, Pete I'll call him.

The consensus we reached that evening was that men are afraid of anger, especially a woman's rage. Pete said a woman he had just begun dating said she could get very angry when provoked. "That scared me," he confessed.

"Why does it scare you?" I said.

David interjected, "Because men are afraid of their *own* rage. I mean, look at what it's done." Good point. Ninety-eight percent of violent crimes are committed by men. And of course there is that darned, ever present male-driven spectacle—war. So maybe when men see rage they see unfathomable trouble, and historic memory takes over; they fear the onset of an emotion they may not be able to handle without doing damage. Anger, it seems, flags a call for defense, a full-throttle standoff for which they may not be in the mood.

And maybe, when encountering a woman's rage, a man hears his mother's voice and is transformed into the boy who feared her intractable scorn—he dreads being made to feel, again, like the beholden, disappointing son. Whatever the reasons, female anger seems to get translated, in the male mind, with copious amounts of secondary meaning.

I explained that most women seem to know that our rage is simply the momentary expression of one of many human emotions, and that there is no far-reaching, menacing consequences of airing it; aside from feeling as though we may lose, for the moment, the man at whom it is directed.

"But why do women have to be so angry so much of the time?" they asked in unison. "Can't they just have a civil conversation, with a beginning and an end, so we can have it done with? I am tired," Pete said, "of walking on eggshells; not knowing when or from where the wrath will come."

Right. Some men don't read people that well. So when the

rage arrives, he's off balance, unprepared for the eruption; he didn't pick up the cues leading to it.

"But," I said, feeling lonely, wishing there were another woman present, "only you can define the ground upon which you walk. You say you want it resolved, but it sounds like what you want is for it to be *over*, done with like a bad toothache. You guys want so-called resolution within the seven minutes you are willing to allocate, before you pack up your sneakers and head for the gym. If it can't be fixed within a precise window of time, you tune out and curse the constant fury of women. And besides," I added, stating what seemed like an obviosity, "anger is part of life; it certainly is a part of mine."

"But why," they both wanted to know, "does the anger last so long? Women cling to it for weeks, months. . . . They *like* it. We don't."

"Because it is NOT resolved. We're waiting for an understanding to kick in. How do you guys walk away so easily from unfinished business?"

"We think it's finished."

At this point I am stupefied. I begin to lack faith in the purpose of our conversation. Nevertheless I continue striving, as is my wont, for mutual lucidity.

"Don't you think women pick up on your edginess, of wanting it done with? You try talking to someone who's checking his watch every three seconds. That in itself is maddening. We feel hurried, unheard, and slightly immoral because we want more time and better attention. We know resolution comes slowly, with a good deal of listening and talking and heated exchange. This is NOT A BAD THING," I say, fuming, sounding like one of the berserk women they find so fearsome. "The intolerance of men to deal with our rage begets more fury," I find myself saying *really* loudly.

While the men at the table were cheering each other on in their righteous oblivion, I was thinking: If men are afraid of anger, *imagine the places they will not go for fear of running into it,* like any kind of situation or conversation that is not predominantly friendly, thus excluding a hefty portion of all meaningful human interchange. They will chuckle instead, heading off the nasty tangle of a deeper quest. Or they will avoid revisiting a childhood, where a mighty rage was once born and has been simmering since. (Denied rage often parades around in outré, clumsy disguises, such as teasing, verbal assaults, enforced silence, and megalomania.) A man will dodge conflict, and maybe even the truth, in order to steer clear of imminent wrath—a high price for short comfort, and a sure way to keep everyone steamed.

"I am convinced that the best way to deal with anger," I say calmly to the men, offering an olive branch, "is to confront it, play it out, and then move on. Really. Not to tiptoe around it, or plot a wily getaway. I am reminded of a Robert Frost line that goes something like: 'The best way out is always through.' Y'know? It's true. I mean, if you don't deal, it goes somewhere. The rage has to settle somewhere. *Repressed* anger is what you should fear, now *that's* scary."

"Through what? Out of where? And why?" Pete asks rhetorically.

"Oy," I say, shredding my napkin. And I mumble something like the golden secret to world peace lies hidden somewhere in between men and their anger; and that teaching boys to fearlessly coexist with the full scope of their emotions is the place to start.

5

Being a woman is a terribly difficult task since it consists
principally in dealing with men.

—JOSEPH CONRAD

Traversing male nation without girlfriends is, for me, unthinkable. Mostly, it's the humor, our cozy lampooning of common ordeals, that gets me through. I met Merrill over twenty-five years ago in my grandmother's kitchen. Across the succotash and pan-fried fish, we traded knowing silly glances (over what I cannot recall) and we have been friends—speaking, listening, and laughing in sisterly symmetry—ever since. When we meet we talk as if we are weaving an eternal cloth, picking up where we left off; and we are locomotive—finding a path and composing at a rate only we two know.

One Sunday late in the summer several months ago, I stole a day and visited Merrill at her house in the country. We walked to the water, about a mile away, swam halfway across the lake (I have in later years overcome most of my fear of water), then flopped onto the sandy shore and slept in the sun for nearly an hour. We walked back home, in towels and suits nearly dry by now, then took a ride up to the bay, and wolfed down chili dogs and vanilla shakes. It was, in just about every way, a balanced, perfect day—uncramped by time and particulars. Some of the time, we talked about men.

"I was thinking," she said, gathering her wet long hair into a knot, "about my ideal man. Y'know, a kind of montage of the qualities I'd love in a guy."

"And . . . ?"

"He's me."

"Do you think he exists?"

"No," she said, smiling and dunking.

"I always feel like, no matter how patient and kind a man is, that while we are engaged in personal talk, I am keeping him from cutting down trees or checking the scores. It's like he's taking the fifth position [in ballet], angled toward the door, in a getaway stance. It's a definite intimus interruptus kind of thing. If the discussion gets too messy, he starts talking to the cat, or says something obtuse, and then when I call him on it, he pleads sincerity, like he's really concerned about whether there's gas in the car. It's like they're loitering outside the torture chamber, killing time because they sense they're gonna get hurt if they linger too close too long."

"Well, in some instances, intimate talk for them *is* torturous. You know that. And they do get hurt. And sometimes they just can't recover quick enough.

"They seem burdened, exhausted," I said, swimming toward Merrill, who waited for me a few feet ahead. "What seems natural to us, y'know, conversing for a sustained period of time about conflict, doubt, or any subject besides statistically based info topics leaves a guy hopelessly in over his head. It's heartbreaking really."

"I know," Merrill says, adjusting her bathing suit strap. "I'm always torn between wanting to assist him in his escape, because he looks so injured, and being determined to keep him there so eventually he'll get used to it."

I tell Merrill that as a woman I have rarely felt defeated by the power of men (the power of women I knew, both splendid and horrid); rather, I have felt oppressed by a man's inability to handle the tough emotional material, the intimate quandaries that life and relationships are full of. Because when they can't or don't or won't, women must.

"Roger [a friend] once told me that men don't avoid intimate talk, it just takes them longer to get there. They make these little tributaries to ease into the heavy stuff. It's a foreplay thing. He said guys just don't dive into major topics, y'know, without some prepping. I told him women do that all the time, dive in; we'll be talking about our deepest terrors as soon as our coats are off. I think he found that horrifying and slightly distasteful."

"Yeah, but sometimes I think men get lost in the tributaries. And then they don't know how to find their way out," Merrill said, her face pointed toward the sun.

"Right. But when they do talk about meaningful things, and they do, they seem to get through it unscathed, relieved even to have opened up. But they don't remember that the next time. It's the same old fear, each time. It's like they're adding two and two and getting two twos. Again and again," I say. And we laugh.

"What I wouldn't give to be that literal," Merrill sighs. "Not forever, but sometimes. Life would be so much simpler."

And it is true. It's the simplicity I want, for a weekend, anyway—to just hang without being burdened by the hyper-cognition women seem to have. I want to get on with the business of being my man-self. But I keep thinking, I can't do this when no one's minding the nonexact. *Someone* has to intuit.

"But I don't think their lives *are* simpler," I say to Merrill. "They seem harassed or confused so much of the time, because they just don't get it."

"Yeah, but you're saying that because you're a woman," she says after she's come up for air. "You think that matters. I mean, we don't like to be confused, we, at least, want to try to get it. But they're no worse for the wear, seems to me. Half the time I don't think they know they're not happy as clams," Merrill says with heartless irony, eying the shore.

"Do you think our sons will be different?" I ask, swishing my hands through the deep water.

"Hard to tell. Teenagers don't talk much and listen even less."

"I think they will," I say.

"I hope."

"Ummm . . . we're pretty far out," I say, worried, getting tired and glancing at the faraway shore, in water way over my head. Merrill, a seasoned swimmer, knows I am no Esther Williams.

"Here, I'm standing on a boulder," she said, reaching out for me. "I've got you."

6

Traditionally we are taught, and instinctively we long, to give where it is needed—and immediately. Eternally, woman spills herself away in driblets to the thirsty, seldom being allowed the time, the quiet, the peace, to let the pitcher fill up to the brim.

—ANNE MORROW LINDBERGH
A Gift from the Sea

When I was a girl my mother encouraged my inclination to paint, draw, and design, by providing every medium imaginable with which to create. When she became ill, I stopped; my paints dried up, the pastels and brushes got dusty on the top shelf of a bookcase. With no visible reinforcements, I must've felt that I could not lose myself in colors, without losing my self altogether. I would be sane enough for both my mother and me, glued to reality, because it seemed my father would not or could not stand guard while his wife broke down and his children grew. When my mother was well, my father encouraged my creativity; as a jazz musician he knew the value of artful expression. But his failure to stay parental when life got tough has left me with a lingering faithlessness in matters of support, the *male* version, if the weather's not perfect.

I kept hoping that at the end of one long, weary day I'd find a heavy-duty oak of a person into whom I could lean, in whose shade I'd rest; and he would be immovable and comforting, even if the wind shifted; and I would not have to be ever alert and fearful of my imminent tumbling and resentful bruises. "I'll take care of that," a deep voice would assure, "you go ahead and play." My early exit out of innocence into self-reliance had left me with an appetite for self-indulgence and impractical poetry, and for the mythical father's steady support. I realize, now, that that kind of ingenuous trust fall can occur but once; as a kid with a dedicated Dad. I am an adult now, and my father is dead. It's not going to happen.

In his book *The Book of Guys*, Garrison Keillor writes: "[Women] can't take over the world fast enough for me. Let them run everything . . . let guys be artists and hoboes. We are delicate as roses in winter and need to be wrapped in warmth or else we die." But that's what we've been doing all along. Raising and hugging people, keeping house, making homes, running everything. I'm a sucker for a guy with soft petals and hard romance, but for seekers of warmth daily life can be a chilly distraction, and someone, usually a woman, has to face the day. And what, I want to ask, of *our* blue highways, masterpieces, and embraces?

True equality means a division of labor, the pursuit of being human *and* art, because art, as Oscar Wilde said, "is the most intense mode of individualism that the world has known." If two people are in charge of the appointments, the meals, and make big efforts to read the emotional stirrings of intimates (and nurture them too), then both genders can trip the light fantastic, on alternating Wednesdays.

I believe it is a part of my nature to manage, delegate, and focus (as I believe it is a part of all our natures and can be developed), but I'd like to float, uncentered, and have somebody be me at the helm for a time. Like Merrill, I want to explore the literal, the emotionally serviced life. I want someone to decode *my* moods, to clarify and take care of my relationships, I want to practice benevolent disengagement. I like concreteness as much as the next guy, and I'd love to pass through the day without being leashed by a wide-angle vision and an exhaustive sensory understanding; but I am forever feeling as if I don't have the time, space, or standbys to get there before supper.

My friend Eleanor is fond of saying, "Hey, I take people at face value." But really, she speaks in the hopeful tense here. She'd like to, the relief would be welcome, but no one decodes nuance as fiercely as El does—she can read people, their words and hidden meaning, with uncanny precision. She can't help it; she intuits and detects, as if unalterably programmed for megaperception, not unlike many women I know. (Maybe that's the deal with sex between men and women. It is the place where, for the moment, our genders are both intensely useful and irrelevant—we are detached from our busily scanning brains, and men are free of their plodding verbatims. Eleanor, too, has been known to say that during truly rapturous sex one goes deaf, dumb, and blind—for the duration, our gender wiring is wondrously annulled.)

For years now I have been saying that by the age of fifty I expect to be residing in a silent, fluid solace, beyond words; I will be designing colorful tiles or shaping vases of clay somewhere serene, a return to the art of my girlhood. Only recently have I realized that I hold this imagined plan close as a long-awaited reward, after the continual care of others, finally, joyfully lost in imaginative self-absorption.

Now I am trying to perfect a youthful indifference. I like the line in the British movie, *Wish You Were Here,* uttered by the frowned-upon sassy teenage girl: "Up your bum," she says with perfectly chipper abandon when she meets the disapproving eyes of townsfolk. I'd like to master that sentiment, but I have years of programming to overcome. I have been all too ready to administer balance at a moment's notice, when the slightest need arose of when I *thought* it had arisen.

The true yield of the women's movement may be the realization that women have a right to make art and be happy, without feeling like guilty heretics if everyone else around them is not happy *first.* Removing the presumption that we have to trade big to serve ourselves may free us to bask in our self-consideration without being burdened or distracted by the stigma.

And the most significant benefit of the men's movement may be for men to consider themselves and others with an intimate care that has not been innately driven or generally evident in the past. The great equilabrator can be the humanist cause, which really is no cause at all. Humanism is the ultimate anti-ism—unorganized, unofficial, rhetoric-free; it is a sensibility marked only by the deep, defiant hum of democratic hope heard in between the words and the slow, sure motion toward higher ground.

At the age of forty-five, I am sashaying into the middle of middle age, loosening up my reflexes, taking my time. I'm looking for a liberation not based on or ignited by rescue work while *trying* to develop an unalloyed belief that the males around me will and can take over. I keep practicing that line in the British movie and others, like: "I'm going to play now. To hell with you all. Toodles."

7

Dave Barry writes, "The truth is, guys don't have any sensitive innermost thoughts and feelings. It's time you knew."

Okay. Sometimes we do. We know. But it is always a horrific thud, a lonesome awakening, when we feel we have been cultivating barren, seedless soil or coaxing an unyielding crop—when all our excavating, prompting, listening, and patient training feels for naught, or at least unwelcome. But we try because it's been good for us . . . we women love our talk and treasure its cure, so we assume guys would love it too. We believe our relationships with men could work so much better if only they would pay as much attention to them as we did. Fact is, some guys just don't want to go that deep or wide; and we the women are left feeling like pushy fools when it dawns on us that we have been cajoling our men to go places they'd simply rather not be. A good friend once told me he thought most of life was a mystery and that's just the way he liked it. Hard to believe, we think, that enough comfort or happiness could be found at a baffling distance from what really matters (to us, anyway)—one's innermost thoughts and feelings. But there you have it.

The demands of my inherited single parenthood and a teasing sample of imminent freedom have inspired an early retirement from other hard work in male rehab, such as full-hearted attempts to enroll men in remedial soul searching. I will always make turbo-fueled attempts to communicate; I know no other way. But, as a woman in mid-adult life, I have surmised that there is powerful resistance in mid-adult men, too often defeating and useless; and that there is work to do. But it is not mine.

If a man has not been raised to believe in the riches of reflection and talk; or if he does not possess an inner-driven interest in transformative discovery, an imposed (read: female-driven) rebirth will forever be arduous and contingent, and most likely irritating and exhausting, for both. Grown men, after all, have already been brought up. We ought not to feel as though we can redo (or undo) the blueprint. We can prune, weed, and water, but we cannot plant forsythia where evergreen grow.

It is in growing boys we find the garden worth harvesting. Borrow a boy if you don't have one . . . a nephew, a student, a stepson, a neighbor, a grandson, and show him the way. Appeal to his humanity, ask him daily how he feels and don't let him answer with "I think . . ."; tell him you know the world is unfair but that doesn't mean he should be. Don't ever, ever laugh *at* him, and if he tells you he needs a father to be a man (and that you, his mother, can't show him the way), tell him you know that the absence of any child's parent hurts, but that if he can be his own true self, the rest will follow; and while you admit he resides somewhere close to the center of *your* universe, he may not necessarily hold a similar address among the general population. Hug him tightly and often, and direct him to the dishes.

Surely there are differences between male and female children, but biology is a weak reason to do or not do anything when raising people; it does not deserve our deference. My friend Janet, the mother of three grown girls and a small boy, observes the differences daily. In a recent letter, she wrote: "John [her son] is driving me nuts. He's into this destructive phase that only boys seem to do so well—let's see how this doesn't work!!! Let's see how far I can push this before it breaks??? If this information is so important, why don't they just ask? Some people seem bound to go through life apologizing because it's preferable to asking first. If you ask, the answer might be no. So just do whatever you want and if it doesn't work out you can say you didn't know. Now this seems like a uniquely male behavior to me. What do you think?"

I think it is primarily male behavior; then again, as a kid I dismantled my share of objects. And when my frustrated brother complained to our mother that I had demolished yet another of his possessions, she comforted him by saying: "Don't take it personally. She does the same with her own." And I did. I plowed ahead with abrasive inquisitiveness; I had little regard for things intact.

All of Janet's daughters played varsity basketball, and work hard on the farm their mother built—they are frightfully capable, confident young women. And while Janet witnesses with humor variations in gender, I cannot imagine she will customize her expectations of John because he is a boy, any more than she indulged her daughters because they were girls.

When my sons were little, I made it clear: if they were going to do boy things they were on their own. And they did. They made guns from paper towel rolls, and swords of wood and curtain rods. I did not favor the behavior, but I could ignore most of it, in small modified doses.

According to recent research compiled by the National Institutes of Health, the low level of the hormone serotonin in male primate brains could be the reason human males lack insight, empathy, and sensitivity. The lack of serotonin, the research claims, blunts his feelings, thus diminishing the pain he might feel when he separates from his troop. Female primates, on the other hand, are going nowhere, so they can handle all kinds of emotion. The researchers suggest that the hormonal disparity between male and female primates is undoubtedly true of humans. Maybe. But we are an evolving species and have, over the centuries, learned to question, alter, and adapt our primitive brain chemistry in order to thrive in a civilized society. If we concede to hormonal differences, we promote the calcification of inferior distinctions. The next step becomes the easy, damaging release of boys and girls from the only difference that truly matters—their individuality. We should be telling our kids: Be all you can be, join humanity. As parents, we can disavow the worthless gender differences and celebrate the relevant but few ones.

Raising sons has made very clear to me, finally, how much reorganizing I am willing to do with men, who must unravel their egos and ids on their own. My supply of nurturance is finite and I would rather feed a future generation with the resources I have, the boys who have a right to the mothering, than to labor with a man's often arrested, defiant development, his restless entry out of his I-frame. My crusading, in matters of men and their emotional rehabilitation, has ended.

I have discovered I love a man who can make it through the day without my constant readjustments (I simply disappear when the fumbling gets torturous); and whose enduring sexiness dwarfs most of the aggravation he incurs—his profile in the dark still makes me shiver. He is a man who earmarks articles he thinks I'd like to read, calls my attention to music worth hearing, listens to all of what I write and most of what I want to say, and lets me know honestly what he thinks. And he is willing to see the humor in our everlasting conflicts. I recognize, finally, that not far below our impasses lie our respective human frailties—we have that in common; and, to me, he is very arboreal—oakish, really. Plus, Merrill tells me, I shouldn't sweat the dinner extravaganzas: he's cooking, at least, and it's lovingly for me.

As a result, I can begin to cozy up to a desirable selfishness.

Part 7
Manhood

Two or three things I know for sure, and one of them is that no one is as hard as my uncles had to pretend to be.

—DOROTHY ALLISON
Two or Three Things I Know for Sure

1

I do not claim to know the world of men, exclusive to themselves. I don't know how to decode the poetry in the pauses men share; nor do I understand fully the sweaty, inarticulate bonding of games. I often wonder what goes on in the interior of a reticent man—or if there is an interior at all. Some men seem to let their feelings set, like a hot custard, until they cool or are channeled seamlessly into their vast wordless reserve. But what happens to that reserve? Does it eventually explode, atrophy, leak, grow, crystallize; is it repressed, suppressed, eventually expressed, and if so, how? All of the above, I think. But I can't be sure.

We know what manhood is *not:* queers, females, and quiche-eaters. But we do not know, really, what it is. If a boy grits his teeth long enough, holds back his tears, and learns to fight, he'll rid himself of suspicious nonmale impairments. But his manhood will be audited regularly, everywhere, most often by other men.

Males seem to judge each other's maleness with a scourge I have rarely seen in the community of my gender. Writer and observer of manhood John Stoltenberg thinks people "are no more born with manhood than they are born with anxiety about whether they have it." When some men meet each other, they (unconsciously) make contact with their respective crotches as if to say, I have one too, or I'd like you to meet . . . It's an organ identification moment. Because conventional masculinity is such an unnatural, punishing pose, men seem to always be self-consciously measuring their own to make sure it is not less than it should be. For this reason, and perhaps a few dozen more, some men are more at rest in the company of women. Except in the constant company of strong women, in which some men often seem very, very tired.

Sometimes I see men as perplexed fumblers trying to put together a picture puzzle but some of the pieces are missing and they don't think to look under the bookcase. They get steamed, and eventually they flood with exasperation, thus limiting a further fruitful search for the pieces. The puzzle remains woefully incomplete. The guy settles, gradually, unconsciously, for a flawed picture; but it's better, in his mind, than revisiting that awful frustration (an unmanageable emotion), and the prospect of failure.

Some men are often very good at what they *do*, but less good at who they *are*. And I know they are confused. They want to be sensitive because of the reverberating feedback—mostly from women—that they're not. But then the men's movement gets mad because their own have let the gender pendulum swing too far to the soft side. Rediscover the deep masculine, they bellow, as men are just finally landing a shaky foot in the terrain of emotions. How can one *rediscover* what may never have been? Maybe what we mean to say is that men ought to create themselves *for* themselves, instead of knee-jerk reacting to social imperatives—from brute to wimp and back again.

Guys sometimes seem like boys stranded on the quicksand bank of a stormy river, with no way or scant courage to get to the other side. They are left slipping, sinking, unsure how, when, or if they want to risk traversing the perilous waters. We, the women who share their lives, sense a reluctance in our men to take the leap, as if they are waiting for instructions or a laying on of hands. We respond. It doesn't work. It's not the right voice, ours are the wrong hands. We keep trying, they keep taking. They stay unanointed. We get spent.

But some of the funniest people I know are male. Much of teenage boy humor cracks me up—the witty, dark, acutely observed kind. It reveals an irony that only a person on the brink of preposterousness would see. Boys play fast and loose with their comedy; their humor is often less cautious, more global than the humor of girls their age. They have the freestyle awarded the alleged unoppressed.

My oldest son is fond of agitprop (agitation-propaganda, a phrase popularized in the sixties by filmmaker Melvin Van Peebles), which means making a scene for the sake of a message. Recently, José and I walked into a small food store and he asked, in an attention-getting volume, "Would you still love me if I had AIDS, Mom?" People look, at first uncomfortable, then they see me sighing and shaking my head, and smile because they have teenagers too. He likes to tweak people out of their surface personae and leave a thought behind.

Another time, we shared a sandwich in a restaurant at a table across from two zaftig women. While José observed the diners, he and I conversed. "How's your sandwich (treadmill)? Mine is good (aerobics)," he said, inserting subliminal remarks in his conversation. "José . . ." I whisper, discouraging his for the most part inaudible commentary about the unsvelte diners. But he knows I know he has a core-deep kindness, and that he is one of the few people I know who is utterly free of bias. Despite my hushing, he knows no one makes me laugh as hard or as often as he does.

I find the wit in men that is informed by a bittersweet self-awareness especially appealing, touching, sexy. And because I am more heterosexual than not, I happen to think no one can slow-dance quite like a man. (Though I have happily and impressively lindy-ed with women.)

In the past I have said that what I do not like about men is that they're not women. But that is not true. I love many things about the community of women but I don't want to join it. I am as claustrophobic in tight academic feminist circles as I am in a rowdy men's sports bar. My gender, in both milieus, becomes oppressively pertinent.

In addition, the words we use are often unconsciously subversive. For instance, "diversity" has come to mean an amalgam of races, genders, and cultures. The implication being that race, class, and gender, above all, are what make us different. In so doing, we are affirming that the distinctions which we claim should be insignificant are indeed significant—incongruous, in fact, and disparate. True diversity is a gathering of distinct individuals, who may be secondarily of varied backgrounds, sexes, and cultures. Of course there are experiences unique to blacks, whites, men, women; we are not one big, happy, blurred family. But those differences, for the individual, are subordinate. A gay white male and a black female, for instance, may be far less diverse than, say, two men of the same race who have dissimilar sensibilities and tastes.

Too, I think, if we began to refer to the gender that we are not as the *other* gender, we could allay the antagonism and polarity that the phrase "opposite gender" strongly suggests. To continually represent the other gender as opposing is too much like perpetuating a tired war-between-the-sexes gag.

In our language we are category-crazed; we lazily cling to census-specific info as if it were the bottom-line benediction for our unique selves.

Once, when he was seventeen, José announced to me that he did not want to grow up. I seized with a mother's dread, recovered, and said, "Well, José, you're male. The chances are good."

"No, what I mean is, I don't want to become everyone else's idea of an adult. I don't want to give up my art, music, wear a suit, sell out," he said.

"Sounds good, but," I insisted, "selling out is one thing. Compromise and responsibility are something else altogether."

"Of *course*," he said as if I had missed his point. "I don't think they are mutually exclusive."

I don't really know if a parent can truly affect to any measurable degree a child's destiny or the kind of adult he will be. I've always thought that good parenting didn't matter much; that bad parenting did. (The power we have is to *not* screw them up.) The older my kids get the more convinced I am that the best service we can hope to provide is comparable to that of a good motel experience. While they are en route to adulthood, we are their innocuous Travelodge. We can try to make their stay safe, clean, unintrusive, and low-cost, allowing them the comfort to feel at home, to be themselves—whatever that may be.

Maybe one day my sons will go racing off to babeland, seeking the coy and brainless among us, free at last of matriarchal zeal. Maybe, once they are out of sight, they will find a cozy fraternity in the Marines at home among real men finally, or vote Republican. But I don't think so. Besides loving them, I like them both very much. And though I remain theoretically agnostic regarding the divine purpose of a parent, I am devout in practice. I don't know any other way to be. Though I have tried.

On bad report card days, when I had bottomed out with disappointment, I would affect a swift retreat. "Hey, it's your life,

I'm out of it," I say and then get abruptly silent. My kids look at each other, and then at me, taut and percolating. They are utterly unconvinced of my professed secession, and wait for me to erupt into the sermonizing they know I can't harness. "Right. This will last, we're guessing, six minutes," José says.

And then I burst. "It's fine with me if you want to flip burgers for five dollars an hour for the rest of your life . . . Can't you see you're narrowing your choices? I can't make you do your work, but I can keep you from doing everything else in this house. No TV until June. I'm *not* kidding. . . ."

"Okay, *two* minutes. Mom, face it, you just can't do it."

And it is true. I can't.

If a chance exists of being able to guide a child's life, I take that chance for all it's worth. Then at least I will have given myself the unalterable comfort of knowing I embraced the gamble, for better or worse.

But I cannot and will not help my sons hunt for manhood because I don't know what it is. All *I* can do is raise my kids as people, with an eye on the trials and rituals they will face just because they are boys. My job is to make my sons feel lovable, comfortable in their skin, give them a sense of belonging, and the courage to be individuals. I can help them realize their humanity, but I do not know how to make men of them.

2

*Give us the man, shouts the multitude, who will step forward
and take responsibility. He is instantly the idol, the lord, and the
king among men.*

—BURNAP

But I admit to lapses of wanting to eagerly believe in mythical
manhood. Sometimes I even think I've seen it.

The night Cal Ripken, Jr., broke Lou Gehrig's record of
most consecutive big-league games played, I had been out with
the "girls" (a Wednesday night ritual we have maintained for the
past sixteen years). So I came home, after having discussed and
resolved significant matters of the day, and walked into the living
room where David had been watching the game and subsequent
celebration of what I immediately thought was a truly trivial
pursuit. I've always enjoyed baseball (a result in part of my father's contagious affection for the game); I like the vigorous full-
bodied spin of a man swinging hard into a ball, racing for a base,
and the aesthetics especially of Fenway Park, green and small, the
smells of roasted peanuts and grass. But the infinite interest in
record-breaking minutiae, I never got that part.

David said Ripken had received a twenty-two-minute-and-
five-second ovation from the crowd in his hometown stadium.
Now, there are some things over which to hoot and holler for
this side of a half hour but, as far as I was concerned, showing up
to play a boy's game year to year is not one of them. Baseball
fans, I thought to myself, are peculiarly wed to the inconsequen-
tial numbers. Still, I sat and watched as Ripken tipped his hat at
shrieking fans dangling over the infield walls. But beyond the

pandemonium, past the din of a boisterous crowd, there seemed to be a man of stunning self-possession.

On his way to the microphone under the lights on the field, during the post-game ceremonies, Ripken moved with assurance and grace between his parents. He and his father did not touch, but Ripken eventually clutched his mother around the shoulders and hugged her. I could not take my eyes off this tall, powder-blue-eyed, easy-smiling man.

His speech to the crowd that night was a twentieth-century American family hymn, in both what he said and did not say. He began by paying dutiful homage to the stern, angular man who stood behind him, his father, who he said taught him to play the game of baseball "the right way." But he did not acknowledge any lessons beyond the business of baseball. He turned to shake his father's hand, a perfunctory, distant grip.

Then he paid tribute to his mother. "My mom," he sighed. "What can I say about my mom?" as if words alone could not convey all that she had meant and continued to mean to him. "She is an unbelievable person. She let my dad lead the way on the field, but she was there in every other way . . . she's always been my inspiration." Ripken proclaimed gratitude for and recognition of his mother's compelling influence, "for leading and shaping the lives of our family."

Then he thanked another baseball player for "his example" and for being a "friend."

He concluded his brief speech by mentioning "the most important person—my wife Kelly." He thanked her for her friendship, advice, and the joy she had brought to him. Then he addressed his children, "You, Rachel and Ryan, are my life." Not *baseball?* This was when his mother cried. (Presumably grateful and assured, he had brought love and respect with him into his marriage and family.) The two women hugged. And then Cal and Kelly hugged each other, really hugged each other. They looked each other in the eyes about as deeply as anyone could bear. But no one was hugging Cal Ripken, Sr., who remained reticent, stranded outside the circle of euphoria, his arms fastened closely to his sides. He was a stranger among relatives, poignantly adrift, feeling maybe for the first time that baseball wasn't enough; and that being away from home all those years was painfully too much.

After wanting to turn off what I initially deemed inordinate hype, I found myself silenced and moved by the speech, by the man. I was thinking, Two words: Clone Cal. He was oddly integrated, not one kind of man. He spoke with easy emotion, modesty, and gratitude. His address was not the usual cliché-ridden, hale, hearty-good-fellow, all-for-the-game tribute. He seemed to say it all, by saying very little, well and simply.

In the weeks following his canonization, I was torn between wanting to read everything I could find about Ripken and not wanting to find out he was less than the hero being celebrated that night. I found out that the "friend" he thanked in his speech is a black man; he has poured time and large amounts of money into a foundation that promotes literacy, and he was once the well-received keynote speaker at Howard University, a black college. The morning of the Big Day, the night he was expected to break Gehrig's record for most consecutive games played, he took his daughter to school. Why, of all days? Chris Wallace, the interviewer, asked.

"She was excited about the first day of school. So was I. We all were. I wanted to be there with her." And with baseball legends, including Joe DiMaggio, and the President of the United States in attendance, he chose his kids to throw out the game ball. Immediately after he broke the record he went to the stands to hug his family; he reached for his son and held him close, as if reminding himself and everyone watching that this—a father with his child—is, above all, what counts.

There were pictures in magazines, of him with his arms wrapped around his daughter, stories about how and why he became interested in baseball. "I'd go to the ballpark because I wanted to spend time with [my Dad]. Looking back on it, the thirty minutes when we drove to and from the park made the whole day." He wrote in his yearbook, in deference to his father who never made it to the majors as a player, that his greatest ambition was to be a minor league baseball player. When Ripken is quoted as saying he "learned from his father's example," you know he means he learned what not to do as much as how to play a game. For Ripken, despite wanting to go out and play baseball every day, "there is more to life."

This is a man who has been able to bring dignity to his father's work while reinventing his own dreams, and who was not afraid, finally, to eclipse his dad. He's a man who pays unabashed and heartfelt homage to his mother, by placing his family at the center of his happiness; a man who has stamina, fearlessness, and a sense of commitment. He's no banner-waving family values man, no politician, no speechifying leader. But by virtue of what he *does*, and who he is, he has become an unlikely social activist. He inspires adulthood.

I could say this is a common man, with uncommon character, which he is. But what is so affecting about Cal Ripken, Jr., is that he is a throwback, the legendary man of the fifties we wanted to believe existed. The version that never was. He's the calm, proud Rockwellian man, lanky, strong, honorable, and tender, who loves his mother, respects his wife, honors his father, cherishes his kids. He is a hard worker and reliable provider, a man who assumes responsibility with stunning ease. Those of us who observe him—the reverent media, his cheering fans, women holding back tears, men with radiant, proud grins, and incredulous kids—bring our battered but resilient hope for the rare and inspiring mythical man to *him*. We lay our yearning at his feet, and he humbly obliges. But even as we savor the heroic moment, we are not completely fooled. Cal is only human. That is why we cry.

Part 8

Persons

It is possible that among all these changes individuality may again have a chance to appear, and young men and women may again think of themselves first as persons, and second as members of a sex.

—MARGARET MEAD
Males and Females

1

Slowly and with caution, over the next few years, José and James began to open up, just as my younger son had promised. They returned with their hearts and secrets. I met their girlfriends, we discussed monogamy, and often with irony and insight the meaning of their impending manhood.

When my sons were young, I used to think I might be the kind of boyfriend's mother no girlfriend deserved. Given a mother's protective devotion, I wondered if I would be ruthlessly critical, possessive, no-holds-barred hostile. But when my sons' romantic interests first started to appear, I was relieved to find that, if anything, I liked and magnanimously welcomed any girl who liked my son. I felt an easy, genial affinity.

Maybe mothers are apprehensive about girlfriends because we know that the women our sons love and eventually choose are often our sons' interpreters. Traditionally, females have been the ones in a couple who decode the emotions that concern them both; they have taken the lead in talk; and, God be merciful, they will be the ones who will deconstruct the damage and dubious effects their lovers' mothers have wrought (and will vocally suffer the lack of lessons they failed to teach).

But by the time they came of age I believed in my sons' abilities to decipher their own psycho-emotional influences. I knew they would probably do as much of the talking and bring as many insights into their intimacies as their female partners would be inclined to share. So I felt that not only were they more than capable of interpreting themselves but their mother would be firmly represented in the ongoing analyses too, and by some-one who was there—an inherent loyalist to boot. I was gratefully surprised to realize I felt nothing but faith—deferential, unpos-sessive—regarding their personal relationships.

A few months ago, when I visited my older son, away at school, we wandered into a drugstore. Furtively, respectfully, euphemis-tically I asked if he had what he needed to have "a safe social life."

"Sex, you mean, Mum. Safe sex?" he said rather loudly, patting me on the back. This from the boy who, a mere few years ago, could not bear having his mother and The Word in a room at the same time.

And he began to show signs of advanced scruples.

When I first had kids I had an ingenuous bordering on daft belief that if I treated my kids fairly and with decency they would treat me likewise. It did not take long to figure out that the responses of the opportunistic (i.e., kids) are not driven by an urge to provide in-kind care.

But as José turned the corner into seventeen I began to see a budding thoughtfulness, heretofore unaccountable. I noticed he began to be bothered when he saw I was worried, concerned primarily with how it might feel to be the worrier. During a particularly contentious day for James and me, José was moved to ease the tension. I heard him tell his brother to go easy on me, that "Mom has to worry about all of your problems and my problems too. And I assume she has some of her own. . . ." He started to alter his behavior and make choices based on consideration for others. I heard him tell someone he didn't do drugs because his mother was Carry Nation incarnate and he'd rather be hit in the face ten times than deal with his mother's guilt tripping.

(Having been the child of a mentally ill mother had fine-tuned an already ripened indignation regarding the use of mind-altering substances; I had watched her exist in an unending altered state, under the cruel influence of a biochemical inter-loper. I turn into a terrorist of temperance when it comes to drugs or alcohol. I want to start slapping people around when they are willfully impaired. I want to say, "The Lord above gave you a functioning brain. Why do you want to toy with it?" I realize this is reactionary, and someday I hope to accept a person's reasonable wish to get giddy and vague. But I have never taken for granted the gift of a rational mind; and I certainly did not want my children to trifle with their developing psyches, which were still, too often, irrational.)

Despite José's claim that I had shamed him into sobriety, fact is, I've never skillfully or wittingly employed guilt as a catalyst. I'm far too confrontational. When my teenage son cited me as the reason for his abstinence, he was referring, I think, to the feelings he gave himself when he felt he was betraying a loved one. His mother's words, the ones that had resonated for him and perhaps had finally made sense, had begun to take residence within. And, more importantly, after he had freed himself of the prevalent social suggestion, maybe he realized that getting cloudy was just not for him.

In the months before their perceptible maturity, I would look at my sons and wonder: When will they get it? Have they gathered no moss, no wisdom at all, have all my words and lessons slid into the abyss? Did nothing adhere, were they nonporous units all along? Was my notion of parenting—that I could make a difference through my aching faith and painstaking guidance—vain and inflated from the start?

And then one day I see what I think may be glimmers of accrued and applied good sense, and startling compassion. They begin to make surprisingly sound decisions; they consider precaution and restraint that even we the adults hadn't thought of; they keep themselves safe and healthy, without prompting or reminders; they fully imagine, without self-interest, another's life, and cleaning the sink was *their* idea. Then, in an epiphanous instant, my worn-down hope finds calm freedom. I breathe. I believe they will be all right, and maybe even better than that.

On his way to seventeen, José was becoming aware of the self-sacrifice adults made in the interest of a child's well-being, his. He was developing a conscience. And again, but differently, years later I felt that having been fair and decent just may have mattered.

Merrill once told me of the time she attended the wedding of a friend's son. As toasts were being made, the groom stood, raised his glass to his mother, and said: "Mom, I just want you to know, I heard everything you said." Really, that's all we ever wanted.

2

I do not call myself a feminist, though at times it could be said that I am a female chauvinist. My personal affinity is with women; much of what is important to me—talking, reflecting, fighting for kids, and an endless curiosity in people—I find mostly among friends who are female. And when a man calls himself a feminist, I feel like I do when an invasive neighbor has all the answers to my wilting pansies. I am grateful for his intentions but immediately want to redirect him to the ruin in his own yard.

I have always felt that there was something incomplete in the avowal of one's feminism. But I am as fond of women as I am a fan of boys; and I am not sure I can explain this, except to say that I am instinctively moved by the plight of both. After having raised sons, I am reminded of exactly what's missing in the word—the compellingly common denominator of a far-reaching hope. You cannot make it through the experience of mothering boys without observing the spirit-murdering inequities levied against male children just because they are male children, without seeing how the programmed enslavement of boys plainly and directly informs that of the other gender. Gender oppression is not separate, but equal, and chronically enmeshed. One cannot closely behold a growing boy, especially from a sister's immediate view, without feeling outrage at the abject stupidity of all gender contrivances. I am infuriated by the dense assault of sexism, but before I ever felt disparaged because of *my* gender (that came later) I had become susceptible to the scent of pain unique to boys; my small brother's ache is fixed in my heart.

Watching a bullied boy stoically forge a brave face to mask his tenderness, or to distract his challengers from the smell of his fear, sickens me. A boy would cry if he could, run away, or try to talk it out—if at that moment, in front of other boys, he could be a person instead of a gender, instead of a boy's boy, instead of having to prove he is not a girl. If he could be himself.

My sons would tell me—long after the fact, sometimes years later, because they said they knew I'd get upset—of fights and attacks they tried to avert, had to react to or else. And I have seen out of the corner of my eye the dares they knew they'd have to meet with an aggression alien to their natures. I reacted every

204 ■ IN THE COUNTRY OF MEN

time, nearly unconscious with rage. "Don't play," I'd say. "Do you see how *dumb* that is?" They knew and agreed; but they'd say I didn't understand, it was a boy thing, an initiation into a sub-culture I didn't get, couldn't ever know.

Masculinity is the only club I know whose membership relies on a willingness to endure and perpetrate deeds of indignity. The more vulnerable the boy—the smaller, gentler he is—the more humiliating and unrelenting his initiation will be. It begins when he is cornered in the woods on the way from school in the earliest grades; and continues through collegial hazing, barrooms, boot camp, and killing fields. Ambushed, the young initiate caught in the isolated dark beyond home is expected to prove his honor, by dishonoring his peers, his persecutors; he prevails only by abusing his abusers. A boy who backs down, shows his terror, or pleads reason shames the brethren. And for that he will pay. He will be aggressively harassed and mocked by his challenger and countless others (fight news travels fast), until he settles the score, until he shows he is worthy of a charade in which the oppressed and the oppressor are one and the same. It's much easier to fight, much, much easier than walking away, my kids would say, as if they were talking about a quick awful dose of medicine—a medicine they felt they could neither harmlessly swallow nor safely refuse.

When one of my sons was in the seventh grade I noticed he was watching the sports channel early in the morning before school, while putting his sneakers on and finishing his breakfast. He was never an athlete or a fan, so one day I asked him why he bothered to listen to news about players and games. He said he felt he needed something to talk about with the boys at school; he seemed convinced that what interested him—astral projection, Thelonious Monk, and the history of Mayan Indians, for instance—would be of little interest to his fellow middle-school students. So he would stockpile what he knew would be common, redeemable conversation to get him through the day as a boy. He must've thought that if he talked about what really mattered to him he would be laughed at or, worse, he would be prey. Instead, that year, before he found the courage to be a person, he talked scores, and walked invisibly through the noisy corridors of his school.

I want to tell men to submit their personal reports—to begin by exposing the frightening, small-boy stories of their initiations. I want battle-ruined men to let go of their silent agonies and difficult words. Tell us how empty and broken and forever changed you are because you were yanked from innocence into grisly, bloody combat. As the mother of sons, I need your war stories—intimate and blunt, the truth. So that honor among men can mean a valiant resistance to the violent rites of manhood. I want the dispensing of decorations for brutality to stop.

I never coached my sons in feminist theory—a recitation of the rhetoric is too easily unheard. How can the party line, which advocates equal rights exclusively for women, explain or ease the tyranny of rites unique to boys and men, or the degrading inequality among their own? Feminist doctrine seemed too narrow when compared to the broad sensibility I wished to impart—a way of seeing, hearing, and knowing that perpetually tunes and charges the soul, the lessons that take root long before words, isms, or issues can be understood or debated. An ethos which makes the glorification of aggression absurd, and deems the use of force a moral failure.

My sons have, however, from time to time, noted my fondness for my gender, and an annoyance with theirs.

"It's funny how you, like, hate men, and you have two boys," José would say, half serious, when I would fume generalizations.

"Yeah, but you and your brother are wondrous exceptions," I would say, smiling.

Not one to shirk unqualified homage, he agreed. "Yeah, probably."

Another time when I had bought a book by a refreshingly smart male author about men, I handed it to José and suggested he take a look.

"Yah, right. He wrote the book to get babes," he said.

"I don't think so. I think he's gay."

"Oh. And I should listen to him on the topic, why . . . ?" José, whose favorite gender-bending RuPaul line is that *"Everyone* is in drag," knows exactly why he might like the book.

"Because he knows how dopey alleged manhood is. He's really funny, original."

My sons know I do not hate men (and they know I *really* love one in particular). But they have seen my sad exasperation with gender-based buffoonery—of the male and female kind—and know well my crushing hope for an awakening. Both feminist dogma and patriarchal honor seemed too small to apply to the myriad family concerns we faced—including but not limited to communication, accountability, compassion, their mixed heritage, fatherlessness, and a conscious rejection of ALL roles.

The struggle for selfhood belongs to us all.

3

As they get older, I have not only watched my sons shed the poses and grow closer to their own true souls, but I have seen them fully acknowledge others; though, looking back, I realize they have, it seemed, always recognized me.

Six years ago, for Mother's Day, my thirteen-year-old son José gave me ten gift certificates—all tender acknowledgments of my selfish desires. One was for "one free two hours of peace—reading, coffee, classical music, the couch." Another was for a dinner cooked and served by him. Yet another was for "one free breakfast in bed." Even at what is commonly a self-absorbed age, José was willing to acknowledge my spirit, bearing gifts for a mother, free of centrifugal distractions.

For several years my adolescent sons halfheartedly observed Mother's Day—especially when they were separating and did not want to acknowledge they had one, much less celebrate her existence. They would make a last-minute dash to the 7-Eleven to buy stale carnations and trite cards; and I wanted to say, "Don't bother." But a couple of years ago José made a Mother's Day card to "an incredible mother, and an incredible woman." The priceless gift I'm not sure he knew he gave was his recognition of me beyond *his* place in my life.

My kids have seen some of my artwork—an early watercolor, or a pencil drawing done long ago, all mediocre at best. They have appreciated my quilts, the creations made of a reasonable mix of form and function, and called them art. "Mom is an artist, though she says she isn't," both my sons have been known to insist. And when someone remarks on José's artistic ability (which he clearly inherited from his father), and asks from whence it came, he credits me too. As far back as I can remember, they have dignified, through their generous insight, their mother's unannounced but gestating inclination. Odd that they saw this before I.

When my sons handle the details and say, "I'll take care of that," I float, inflated with faith. When they reveal their hearts and flaunt their empathy I am buoyant, carried by a sense of triumphant fruition.

When I visited José away at school, I was secretly pleased to see a bowl of mints on his table and a list of numbers on the wall over the phone, homemaking details he grew up with and had taken with him.

My younger son has always liked to cook, ever since he designed the top of a pizza in the first year of our three-person family when he was five. When he began to wash dishes at a restaurant when he was fourteen, he would make mental notes about the recipes he watched the cooks prepare, and return home to duplicate them for us. He has said on many occasions, "I'm cooking tonight," and every time I'd feel myself resist an urge to interfere or coach (and very glad that I did), and eventually settle into my chair and contentedly await his presentation; letting it go.

I had always taken my sons grocery shopping with me when they were young and gave lessons along the way: check ingredients, compare prices. Recently when I accompanied José on a food-shopping errand, he pushed ahead with itemized ambition, leaving me on the periphery of the task at hand. He considered price per ounce and used in-store coupons. "Mom, this is definitely a better deal," he said, replacing the box of waffles I had chosen, as I lingered behind in the aisle, gloriously detached. I felt lighter, less the keeper and controller of information I had no personal interest in or yen to continue to know. He was growing into a second-nature detail keeper, doing his part. When my sons do woman's work, we are all that much closer to flight, theirs and mine, and the women's who may share their lives.

As we become more independent, of each other and in ourselves, and I begin to embrace a life separate and distinct from them, I continue to be overwhelmed by their selfless encouragement of the transformation, beyond my mothering. They have never insisted I stay behind, in a role convenient to them; nor do they award me my personal purpose as if it is a favor to give. They assume, as I have of them, my individuality.

4

I had known the ominous burden of having self-absorbed parents and I knew I would NOT be that within sight of my kids. I had decided I would behave with finely tuned consideration above all else, ever vigilant, inordinately capable. Whatever flight of fancy I may have been tempted to chase was instantly grounded by my fear of becoming the unsteady, truant parents I had known as a kid. I would be virtuously consistent.

One day when I was in a funk James, somewhat irked, wanted to know why I was so gloomy. "I have moods too, y'know," I insisted.

"Really? I didn't know," he responded, as if he had gotten news of a radical change in weather. I realized then that I had maintained far too stable a picture of my disposition. They had witnessed my loudmouthed irritation and assertive impatience, but they had not seen me weakened with sadness, vulnerable, or despairing. They saw me sniffle once and that was at the airport because I was so relieved to see José, who had been away for ten days when he was nine. They were tears of joy.

Another time, after I blew up about his failure to make the grade in school, James saw I was distancing, disappointed, and over the top. James came over to me on the couch, put his hand on my head, and said, "You're mad, huh? I'm sorry. Let's cuddle."

"Why are you comforting me?" I fumed.

"Because you look like you need comforting," he said.

"I do, but . . ." I snarled and shooed him away, even more irate.

And yet another time, when I was doling out advice when he was sixteen, James declared, "You know, you don't know everything."

"No kidding," I shot back. And I was thinking, Jesus, you thought even for a second that I did?

We arrived at a balance clumsily—I was a reluctant crossover. As they got older they would push me to the point where they could console *me*, as if they were hunting for my frailty. They were ready to see the whole picture. And eventually I was ready to give it up, to come out from behind the wizard's curtain and be viewed as unceremoniously human. As we had with our made-up myths at an earlier stage, we had agreed, together and without words, to shed yet another fable—a parent's invincibility.

But that is not the whole story. It was not just an unveiling of a parent's vulnerability but the denouement of a cautious daughter in matters of family trust. With a faith in kin I had all but given up for dead, I dared to take their care. I have never felt such trust and terror—to love and be loved so deeply is both unnerving and exquisite.

Their large arms curl around my shoulder, after they sense they have stepped too far, or that I am truly aggrieved or disappointed, and they get warm, steady, and tender. Those hugs are brief, and unremarkable; but they are right, they are the reason—of our mutual life.

———

Even so, I am not naive enough to suppose that my sons will become men free of the irritations I find in other grown males. They will continue to have experiences in a world that I can never know, because of their biology—and they will be shaped, tested, and enlightened by them all. I can only hope they believe that, of all their distinctions, being male is only one and perhaps the least relevant.

But I am reminded of their gender on the rare and spontaneous occasion. For instance, after days apart, sometimes they will do this really weird dance within minutes of seeing each other. James circles his brother, José steps in and back, then they inch toward each other and tangle, spouting dares and exchanging holds, until one gives up. It is a primitive tango, rough and intimate. After having matched muscles, and reestablished a corporeal connection, they emerge relaxed and friendly. A testosterone seizure, perhaps? Maybe they are detonating their hormonal tension. Aside from this brief, contained contest of brawn, both James and José are utterly nonviolent. When they leave each other, they simply embrace. *I* don't get it, but I'm pretty sure it'll pass.

On the other hand, if consigning their combativeness to the infrequent, harmless scramble means they will forgo other more dangerous forms of male aggression—such as crimes of war, abuse, and bullying—and that they can continue to be kind, confident people, I'm all for it. We women have our hormonal backlog too.

There is a picture of James, at the age of five, gleefully anticipating a daring plunge; his tiny body is hanging vertically in the air, his big long curls are suspended in the breeze, and his hands are bent down into a neat diving point. He is beaming straight ahead with fearless joy, en route to the water below.

James and José were strong swimmers from the start. They have never been afraid of the water, even before their abilities matched their nerve. They'd jump into the lake, dunk their heads, and polliwog their way in and out of what would've seemed to me, even now, hazardous depths. Of their early talents, I was most comforted by their brave, easy ability to swim. It was not mine; yet I was assured that, given their confidence, they could swim their way to safety.

As a kid I had no such comfort in the water, and though my father, in trying to soothe my fear and perhaps his own, caused us both to capsize in mutual disillusion, it was not his fault. He had tried to do the right thing. But if James or José had been reluctant swimmers, I don't know if I could have urged my jittery child to climb a towering slide, and then vow to catch him at the end. I'd like to think I would, but I would hedge on the outcome. "I'll try," I'd probably say to my fearful son, "no promises, but I'll give it my very best."

About the Author

JAN L. WALDRON is the author of the critically
acclaimed *Giving Away Simone*. She lives with
her family in New England.

Printed in the United States
by Baker & Taylor Publisher Services